THIS
IS MY
STORY

146 *of the* WORLD'S GREATEST GOSPEL SINGERS

DAVID LIVERETT

with JUDY SPENCER NELON

NELSON REFERENCE & ELECTRONIC
A Division of Thomas Nelson Publishers
Since 1798

www.thomasnelson.com

Unless otherwise noted, Scripture quotations are from the Holy Bible, King James Version.

Scripture quotations noted THE MESSAGE are from *The Message* by Eugene H. Peterson. Copyright © 1993, 1994, 1995, 1996, 2000. Used by permission of NavPress Publishing Group. All rights reserved.

Scripture quotations noted NIV are from the HOLY BIBLE, NEW INTERNATIONAL VERSION®. Copyright © 1973, 1978, 1984 by International Bible Society. Used by permission of Zondervan Publishing House. All rights reserved.

Published by Thomas Nelson, Inc., P.O. Box 141000, Nashville, Tennessee 37214.

Library of Congress Cataloging-in-Publication-Data is available.

ISBN: 1-4185-0607-9

Printed in Canada

1 2 3 4 5 — 09 08 07 06 05

*Dedicated to the memory of Joel Hull
and Zella Hull Warren, from whom I learned
much about God's love and who encouraged me to sing
bass in the choir at the Austinville Church
of God in Decatur, Alabama.*

Old Friends

CHORUS:

Old friends—after all of these years, just
Old friends—through the laughter and tears
Old friends—What a find! What a priceless treasure!
Old friends—like a rare piece of gold
Old friends—make it great to grow old
(brought me in from the cold; Christmas version)

Oh, God must have known
That some days on our own
We would lose our will to go on—
That's why He sent friends like you along.

Old friends—yes, you've always been there,
My old friends—we've had more than our share—
Old friends—I'm a rich millionaire in old friends.

VERSE

A phone call, a letter, a pat on the back,
*   or a "Hey, I just dropped by to say . . ."*
A hand when we're down, a loan when we just couldn't pay—
A song or a story, a rose from the florist,
*   a note that you happened to send—*
Out of the blue just to tell us that you're still our friend

REPEAT CHORUS

Table of Contents

Introduction

y dad always loved good music. Recently one of my cousins was showing me where my dad grew up. Along with my maternal cousin, Joyce, my brother, Edwin, and my wife, Avis, we were traveling the back roads of north Alabama near the village of Anderson. Edwin was making a map locating all the houses that my folks had called home. At one place Joyce said "Here is the place that Uncle Monroe and Mother used to hike through the woods to hear the Grand Ole Opry. They would hurry home and try to imitate the sound." I have an old photo of my dad's family standing out in front of the homeplace; it shows some of dad's fifteen siblings holding musical instruments.

I grew up in Decatur, Alabama, in the 1940s and 1950s, I still remember dad, Buford Brewer, and O. T. Terry making music on our front porch. One of the songs they would play was "I'm Using My Bible for a Roadmap." Dad even rigged up a holder for his harmonica so he could play it while he played the guitar. He and mom bought my brother and sister, Aldena, a Silvertone guitar and a mandolin for Christmas one year. I think it was the same Christmas I received a hand-me-down bike that Dad repainted red. As it turned out, Dad's musical talent died with him. My brother ended up in the space industry and my sister worked in insurance. I am the youngest child, and I leaned toward the visual arts.

When all-night singings were nearby, our family would attend. The singings were usually held at the high school. I don't remember if the concerts really went on all night, but they did leave a lasting impression. My recollection of the singers is that they wore matching suits and had slicked-back hair and pencil-thin mustaches. We would stay to listen through encore after encore. In 1952 we went to the Ryman Auditorium in Nashville, Tennessee. We sat under the balcony and someone spilt a Coca-Cola down onto our pew.

After graduating from Anderson College in Indiana with a major in art, I was hired to create the printed materials for the college and to teach the visual arts class. Not long after that, a college friend of mine introduced me to Bill Gaither just a few years after Bill's groundbreaking song "He Touched Me." Pinebrook Recording Studio, now Gaither

Studios, was ready to open for business and someone was needed to design record jackets for custom projects. For the next few years I designed songbook covers, press kits, and concert information for the Bill Gaither Trio and other groups.

By the time the Homecoming video series began, I had my own graphic arts business and had been away from gospel music for years. I was publishing books and freelancing for a large publishing house. My company had published books on lighthouses, little country churches, and bridges—each with an inspirational theme.

Drawing faces had always been an interest of mine and it was time for a change. On August 1, 2003, I approached Bill Gaither about the possibility of drawing maybe seventy-five singers who had been featured on the video series. My idea was to have a short biographical sketch of each individual across the page from a pen-and-ink drawing. As it turned out, the book has almost doubled in size, and I still wasn't able to include all the singers who have been featured on the videos. It was hard to leave anyone out, but an effort was made to include the original singers that my dad loved so much.

My father, Monroe William Liverett, had a beautiful tenor voice and sang in the choir of the Austinville Church of God in Decatur, Alabama. He died two months before the first Homecoming video was recorded in 1991. Daddy would have loved watching every one. My mother, Elna McConnell Liverett, was also a member of the choir at the Austinville church. She loved singing the hymns of the church. She died in February 1993. Whenever I hear Fanny Crosby's great hymn, "Blessed Assurance," I think of her.

She knew in whom she had believed and upon whose everlasting arms she leaned with such blessed assurance. She was one of the women who had seen the risen Lord and who came to tell the Good News of hope and love. I can hear her beautiful soprano voice singing through time and eternity.

Blessed assurance, Jesus is mine! Oh, what a foretaste of glory divine!
Heir of salvation, purchase of God, Born of his Spirit, washed in his blood.

This is my story, this is my song, Praising my Savior all the day long;
This is my Story, this is my song, Praising my Savior all the day long.

Echoes of mercy, whispers of love.

—David Liverett, July 14, 2005, Anderson, Indiana

THIS
IS MY
STORY

146 *of the* WORLD'S GREATEST
GOSPEL SINGERS

Mary Ann Gaither Addison

January 17, 1945—

The LORD is my shepherd; I shall not want. . . . Psalm 23

I n the mid-1950s a sister and her two brothers—Mary Ann, Danny, and Bill—began singing in small churches and at youth rallies in central Indiana. Their concerts consisted of gospel standards perfected around the family piano. When their voices went out on a daily broadcast, sponsored by the grocery store where Bill worked, what came back was a steady stream of invitations to sing not only at churches but also at fairs, farm bureau meetings, and civic gatherings. To accommodate their audiences, the trio added some secular favorites to their gospel music concerts. Before long they were singing most evenings and every weekend. That family threesome—Mary Ann, Danny, and Bill—was the genesis of the Bill Gaither Trio.

Eventually, the Trio's tour took them beyond Indiana borders to such nearby states as Illinois, Ohio, Michigan, Kentucky, and Tennessee. Mary Ann was barely in her teens when the Bill Gaither Trio made its entry into the world of gospel music. Her deep alto voice was the perfect blend with her brothers Bill and Danny. Mary Ann sang with the Bill Gaither Trio for eight years.

Married to Don Addison, the mother of two children and grandmother of five, today Mary Ann works for the Gaither organization as tour coordinator for Homecoming and Gaither Vocal Band Concerts. Like Bill, Mary Ann still lives in Alexandria, Indiana, near Grover's Corners, the home of their grandfather, Grover Gaither.

In 1999 Mary Ann was inducted with the Bill Gaither Trio into the Gospel Music Association Hall of Fame. As a founding member of the Bill Gaither Trio, she is a pioneer in a musical style often referred to simply as *Gaither music,* still a heavy influence on the music world.

Doris Akers

May 21, 1923—July 27, 1995

And hope maketh not ashamed; because the love of God is shed abroad in our hearts by the Holy Ghost which is given unto us. Romans 5:5

After becoming a Christian, Tim Spencer, an original member of the Sons of the Pioneers, heard the music of Doris Akers and the Sky Pilot Choir of Los Angeles, California. He signed her to RCA Records and Manna Music Publishing.

One Sunday night at the world-famous Sky Pilot Church, just before the choir was to march into the evening service, Doris asked her choir members to pray Heaven down. She described this moment as very special and kept thinking over and over, "there is a sweet, sweet spirit in this place." The next morning she completed "Sweet, Sweet Spirit," which has become a classic gospel song. In 1965 Doris recorded an album that included the song with the Statesmen Quartet for RCA.

In 1993 Doris was invited to a Gaither Homecoming taping. Bill began to play the piano for her to sing her song, "Sweet Jesus." Bill couldn't seem to get the beat the way she wanted it, so she boldly walked over, pushed him off the piano bench, and began to play the beat that obviously only she could play. The Homecoming Friends erupted with laughter, especially Bill who enjoyed that kind of spontaneity which has contributed to the success of the video series.

In 2001 Doris received numerous awards and was inducted into the Gospel Music Association Hall of Fame. The Smithsonian Institute also honored her multiple talents by labeling her songs and recordings "National Treasures."

—Judy Spencer Nelon

Glen Allred

June 19, 1934—

And we know that all things work together for good to them that love God, to them who are the called according to his purpose. Romans 8:28

G len was born Glennan H. Allred in Monroe, Tennessee, the youngest of the three children of Lola Grace and Homer Allred. While still in grammar school, he learned to read music. He remembers "a bunch of cousins who played" and that he "started playing a Gene Autry guitar when [he] was eight years old. It cost a whopping four dollars." When he was fourteen years old, Glen joined the Dixie Drifters, a country band in his hometown, Monterey, Tennessee. The group traveled in a pick-up truck, all four members riding in the cab. On one of their singing dates they opened a program for Wally Fowler and the Oak Ridge Quartet. Wally asked Glen to go to Louisville, Kentucky, the next Sunday to try out for the group. For about a year and a half, in the early 1950s, he played the guitar and sang baritone for the Oak Ridge Quartet. After being cut from the group in May of 1952, Glen left Nashville, Tennessee, and headed to Valdosta, Georgia, where he joined the Happy Rhythm Quartet. Later that year, he was offered a job with the Gospel Melody Quartet. Soon after that, Les Beasley joined the group, and in 1955 they changed their name to the Florida Boys.

Glen has one of the smoothest baritone voices in the business. Besides playing the guitar and singing his unique style, he is considered one of the sweetest and nicest men in southern gospel. Glen has been married to Shirley since 1954. They have two children, Randy and Cindy. He commends Shirley for her strong Christian faith and for taking their children to church all the years that he couldn't be there. He says he could not have made it without the support and faith of his family.

Glen was recently inducted into the SGMA Hall of Fame and appeared on the February 2001 cover of *Singing News*.

Les Beasley

August 16, 1928—

Greater love has no one than this, that he lay down his life for his friends. John 15:13 NIV

es was born Lester George Beasley in Crockett, Texas. As a preacher's kid, Les had plenty of opportunities to sing in church at an early age, and he loved singing with four-part harmony groups. A bad case of measles changed his voice forever.

The Beasley family lived in several places in eastern Texas, Louisiana, and Arkansas. After Les moved from West Helena, Arkansas, to Beaumont, Texas, he joined the Marines just as the United States was entering the Korean War. He saw action in both South and North Korea as part of the First Tank Battalion, First Marine Division.

After the war, Les joined the Gospel Melody Quartet in 1955. The Quartet was soon renamed the Florida Boys. He has managed the group for over forty years. Les is a lifetime member of the board of directors of the Gospel Music Association and served as president for two years. He is president of The National Quartet Convention, which annually promotes the National Quartet Convention in Louisville, Kentucky. Les's son, Clarke, continues the family tradition as director of the National Quartet Convention.

As producer of the nationally syndicated "Gospel Singing Jubilee" program, Les Beasley pioneered gospel music on television.

A committee composed of Bill Gaither, Herman Harper, and Les suggested that the GMA board present an award as part of their annual meeting. Les named it the Dove Award.

Les Beasley believes he is doing what the Lord would have him do, and that has kept him singing these fifty-plus years.

Roger Bennett

March 10, 1959—

Therefore we do not lose heart. Though outwardly we are wasting away, yet inwardly we are being renewed day by day. For our light and momentary troubles are achieving for us an eternal glory that far outweighs them all. So we fix our eyes not on what is seen, but on what is unseen. For what is seen is temporary, but what is unseen is eternal. 2 Corinthians 4:16–18 NIV

Pianist, vocalist, and songwriter Roger Douglas Bennett was born in Jonesboro, Arkansas. At an early age Roger learned to love southern gospel music and enjoyed the harmonies of the Florida Boys, the Kingsmen, the Goodmans, and the Cathedrals, the group he joined in November 1979. Joining this group represented the fulfillment of a lifelong dream for Roger. Singing southern gospel music was truly his desire in life. Roger remained with the legendary Cathedral Quartet until its retirement from the road in 1999.

With Cathedrals' baritone Scott Fowler, Roger helped form Legacy Five, one of today's leading quartets. Over the years, Roger has received many awards presented by his fans and peers, including the Singing News Favorite Pianist from 1993 to 2003 and the Dove Award for Southern Gospel Song of the Year in 1999 for "Healing."

Roger is also a very accomplished songwriter, having penned several singles and number-one songs. Roger comments that his favorite song is "Blessed Assurance," and his favorite self-penned composition is "Whispers in the Night."

Even though his awards are appreciated, the most special and memorable thing for Roger has been the outpouring of love and prayers when he was diagnosed with leukemia in 1995. "My family and I literally depended on God every day to get us through. And God used our musical family to keep us encouraged. Our lives have been touched so much by their love and concern."

Roger and his wife, Debbie, live in Thompson Station, Tennessee, with their children, Chelsea and Jordan.

—Crystal Burchette

Doyle Blackwood

August 22, 1911—October 3, 1974

Thou wilt keep him in perfect peace, whose mind is stayed on thee: because he trusteth in thee. Isaiah 26:3

oyle Jimmie Blackwood was born in a three-room shack on a small farm near Ackerman, Mississippi. His parents, William Emmett and Carrie Blackwood, were sharecroppers. He had two brothers and a sister. Though poor, the family was strong and had a deep religious commitment.

Doyle was fascinated by music even in childhood. Emmett and Carrie recognized their children's musical talent and sold valuable prize chickens to finance music lessons. While the older children were at school, Doyle would amuse himself by singing songs he had learned in church that week. He learned to sing harmonies, play the mandolin, and read shaped notes in Sunday school. He commented, "My first and most lasting ambition was to learn everything possible about singing and then to become a professional gospel singer."

Doyle liked the singing style of the Delmore Brothers and of Jimmie Rodgers. His favorite song over the years was "Turn Your Eyes upon Jesus." In the early years of the Blackwood Brothers Quartet, he accompanied the group on the mandolin and guitar. He was also the original manager and master of ceremonies. He was called the "Mighty Mite of the Mike" because he stood five feet, three inches tall and weighed 102 pounds. He always enjoyed a good joke about his size.

Doyle died in 1974 as a result of complications suffered from an accident at his farm in Hernando, Mississippi. His life was one of service to people and obedience to God. Everyone loved him.

Doyle was married to Carmen; their children are Terry and Karen.

—Charles de Witt

James Blackwood

August 4, 1919—February 3, 2002

Behold, God is my salvation; I will trust, and not be afraid: for the LORD *JEHOVAH is my strength and my song; he also is become my salvation.* Isaiah 12:2

I n 1934 fifteen-year-old James Webre Blackwood joined his brothers, Doyle and Roy, and his nephew, R W, to form a group called the Blackwood Brothers. No one could have known then the impact that the Blackwood Brothers and James Blackwood would have on a fledgling style of music known as southern gospel.

Since it was difficult to make a living as musicians in those days, the group disbanded in 1935. At that time, Roy and R W left their hometown of Ackerman, Mississippi. When they returned a couple of years later, the Blackwood Brothers began singing together once again.

In 1939 James married Miriam (Mim) Grantham in a double wedding ceremony with Doyle and his bride, Carmen. Mim became a role model for other quartet wives as she stood by James, realizing the calling he had from God. They had two sons, Jimmy and Billy.

After World War II ended, the quartet took on a new look for James, R W, and Doyle Blackwood: Bill Lyles began singing bass. The group became famous and made its first television appearance in 1948. In 1952 the Blackwood Brothers were acclaimed as having their best quartet yet when James, R W, and Bill were joined by tenor, Bill Shaw. In 1954 they won the "Arthur Godfrey Talent Scouts" program. Not long after this recognition, a tragic plane crash in Clanton, Alabama, took the lives of R W Blackwood and Bill Lyles. James said he would never sing again; but, after much prayer, he stayed with the group. Cecil Blackwood became the new baritone, J. D. Sumner was the new bass, Bill Shaw was tenor, and Jack Marshall on the piano rounded out the group.

James was inducted into the GMA and SGMA Halls of Fame and won countless awards and honors for his many contributions. He is remembered for singing two songs in particular, "How About Your Heart" and "I'll Meet You in the Morning."

Jimmy Blackwood

July 31, 1943—

But seek ye first the kingdom of God, and his righteousness; and all these things shall be added unto you. Matthew 6:33

I t was 1943 and World War II was raging when James and Mim Blackwood moved to National City, California. There on July 31 Mim gave birth to their first son, James, Jr. After the war the family moved back to Iowa where James, Jr. (Jimmy) began piano lessons at the age of six. In 1950 when the family moved to Memphis, Tennessee, James had hopes for Jimmy to play the piano for the Blackwood Brothers Quartet. In 1962 Jimmy attended the Stamps School of Music in Dallas, Texas, for more piano instruction; to everyone's surprise he sang his first solo. Thus began a singing career that has spanned four decades.

Jimmy met Mona during a youth fellowship outing, and they married in 1963. They have two beautiful daughters and five awesome grandchildren, who "surpass any award man has ever given."

Jimmy sang with the Junior Blackwood Brothers, and as a member of the Stamps Quartet and the Blackwood Brothers, was inducted into the GMA Gospel Music Hall of Fame. The Blackwood Brothers won five Grammys and received numerous other nominations while Jimmy was with them. In 2003 Jimmy and the Blackwood Brothers joined the Jordanaires on Englebert Humperdink's first gospel album, which was also a Grammy nominee.

In March 1984 Jimmy was diagnosed with pancreatic cancer, with a very short life expectancy; but he was miraculously healed. Rev. Dan Betzer wrote the account in the book *Deliverance . . . In the Valley of Death.*

In 1986 Jimmy began a solo ministry, singing and sharing his testimony of God's wondrous healing power. He continues to bless people in his solo ministry and through the reunion of the Blackwood Brothers Quartet. The Blackwoods were pioneers in the gospel music industry, and that legacy continues through the voice of Jimmy Blackwood who sounds a lot like his famous father.

—Mona Blackwood

R. W. Blackwood, Jr.

November 27, 1942—

Ye are of God, little children, and have overcome them: because greater is he that is in you, than he that is in the world. 1 John 4:4

obert Winston Blackwood, Jr. was born in National City, California; by his eighth birthday his family had moved to Memphis, Tennessee. When Winston was ten, his father heard him singing in the car and told him, "You will be singing in the next Blackwood Brothers concert." Not long after that, on June 30, 1954, his father was killed in a tragic plane crash in Clanton, Alabama.

By the time Winston was twelve, he had sung at a Billy Graham Crusade and had won the top award on the national television show, "The Ted Mack Amateur Hour."

As he grew older, Winston lost interest in gospel music and wanted to be a rock star, due partly to the influence of Elvis Presley, whom he had known prior to his father's death. Winston moved to Nashville but had little success with his career. However, he received a call to join other sons of the original Blackwood Brothers to form the Junior Blackwood Brothers.

Winston had not been in church much after his father's death and had never made a commitment to God. In fact, he had been a "big party boy." As the Junior Blackwood Brothers continued to travel and sing the precious songs his father had sung, Winston became convicted. He gave his heart and life to Jesus Christ at a revival service in 1964.

At present Winston, his wife, Donna, his brother, Ron, Ron's wife, Shelley, and two other men have formed the Blackwood Singers. They perform in Pigeon Forge, Tennessee. Winston's favorite song, "His Hand in Mine," is one that his dad often sang.

After their marriage in 1965, Winston and Donna had two children, Andrea and Rob, who have given them seven grandchildren.

R W Blackwood, Sr.

October 23, 1921—June 30, 1954

Let not your heart be troubled: ye believe in God, believe also in me. In my Father's house are many mansions: if it were not so, I would have told you. I go to prepare a place for you. And if I go and prepare a place for you, I will come again, and receive you unto myself; that where I am, there ye may be also. And whither I go ye know, and the way ye know. John 14:1–4

Born in Ackerman, Mississippi, R W Blackwood, Sr. and his brother, Cecil, grew up traveling with their parents, Roy and Susie. Because Roy was an evangelist and church overseer, R W began singing at age three in church and revival services with his father. At eight he was singing tenor in a quartet that his father had formed in the church he was pastoring. Even then R W was a hit. He was able to attend "singing schools" and "singing conventions" all over the South and Southeast. This kind of schooling, where he learned technique, how to read shaped notes, and how to perfect his God-given talent, was R W's favorite. When he would return to the homeplace in Ackerman, Mississippi, he and his Uncle James, two years his senior, would climb a tree and discuss the "singing school" lessons they had learned.

Beginning in 1934 in Ackerman, the original Blackwood Brothers Quartet—Roy (34), Doyle (24), James (15), and R W (13)—traveled around in Roy's 1929 Chevrolet. R W soon finished high school in Ackerman.

R W met and married Elaine in Jackson, Mississippi, in 1939. They had two sons, Ron and Winston (R. W., Jr.). During World War II the quartet was working in the Aurora Aircraft Plant in San Diego. R W was drafted and while serving in Okinawa, he formed a quartet. After the war, the Blackwood Brothers bought a plane, and R W became the pilot. He managed the Brothers, sang baritone, and arranged the group's RCA Victor recording contract and appearance on "The Arthur Godfrey Show."

R W was killed in a plane crash in 1954 in Clanton, Alabama. Jake Hess said that R W was not only "Gospel music's greatest baritone, but prior to his death, he had discussed forming a national quartet convention." Several years later his dream became a reality.

Terry Blackwood

October 21, 1943—

Delight thyself also in the LORD; and he shall give thee the desires of thine heart. Psalm 37:4

ichard Terrell Blackwood was the oldest child of Doyle Blackwood, co-founder of the famous Blackwood Brothers Quartet. He was born in Ackerman, Mississippi, near the Tombigbee National Forest. Terry grew up with one sister, Kay. He believes that his father was the greatest influence on his musical career: "Dad had this consistent integrity." Although his father, Doyle, had become a musical legend, Terry set out to make his own way.

With his distinctive vocal style Terry has received acclaim as a trendsetter with the Imperials and Andrus, Blackwood & Company. With his cohorts, Jim Murray, Sherman Andrus, and Armond Morales, he received many Grammy and Dove Awards during the 1970s and 1980s.

A doctor once told Terry and his wife, Tina, they could never have children. Since then they have been blessed with two sons, Luke and Jesse, and a daughter, Leah Carmen-Marie.

Terry lives in Leiper's Fork, Tennessee, and has an active solo ministry in churches across the country. He performs selected dates with former members of the Imperials in a group called the Classic Imperials.

Along with the Stamps Quartet, the Classic Imperials recently released a new CD called *The Gospel Side of Elvis.* Most of the group members were in the original cast that began with Elvis in 1969 in Las Vegas.

Terry also released a solo CD, *From the Heart,* that features "Shout to the Lord," "So High," and "Somebody's Praying." Many people have been blessed as he has taken this new project to churches across the country. *A Blackwood Homecoming, Volume One* also continues to be very popular with his fans.

Michael Booth

October 8, 1971—

O LORD, thou hast searched me, and known me. Thou knowest my downsitting and mine uprising, thou understandest my thought afar off. Thou compassest my path and my lying down, and art acquainted with all my ways. Psalm 139:1–3

Michael David Booth, the tenor of the Booth Brothers, was born in Tampa and has lived in the state of Florida for most of his life. His introduction to music came through hearing "war stories" from his dad when he sang with the southern gospel group, the Rebels Quartet. His brother, Ronnie, also grew up listening to southern gospel music. Michael became interested in playing the drums and practiced on his mom's pots and pans. He continued to play throughout high school, winning state recognition awards and eventually a jazz scholarship to college.

When compared to his brother, Ronnie, who began crooning at the tender age of five, singing came late for Michael. His first attempt to sing came when he was nineteen years old. Although he had plenty of confidence playing the drums, singing on stage was a different story. Eventually, with lots of practice, his desire to minister through song overcame his fear of being onstage. Fans not only love his singing, but also his natural talent for making folks laugh. What else would you expect from a guy who wrote a song called "Brown Nose in F Major" for his final exam in music theory? By the way, he received an A on the exam!

The Booth Brothers were named the 1999 SGMA New Artist of the Year, the 2002 SGMA Trio of the Year, and the 2004 Southern Gospel News Male Group of the Year.

Michael has had many memorable moments, but the two that stand out are singing with the Cathedrals with George Younce, one of Michael's heroes, and taping a video with Bill Gaither. He says, "God has certainly blessed me with many good things, and the Lord definitely deserves all the glory."

Michael lives in Nashville with his wife, Vicki, and their sons, Christian and Jonathan.
—*Bob Crichton*

Ronnie Booth

June 28, 1965—

Let the words of my mouth, and the meditation of my heart, be acceptable in thy sight, O LORD, my strength, and my redeemer. Psalm 19:14

Fans who hear and meet the Booth Brothers are impressed with the group's unique sound and warm personalities. Ronald Lee Booth II (Ronnie), the lead singer for the group, is one of the big reasons for those impressions. Born in Detroit, Michigan, Ronnie grew up in Tampa, Florida, where the family moved so Ronnie's dad, Ron, Sr., could join the Rebels Quartet. At the age of five, Ronnie sang "The Night before Easter" on the Rebels' television program.

Ronnie's love for music and singing continued to grow during his teens. He immersed himself in a variety of musical styles from such artists as the Rebels Quartet, the Eagles, Barry Manilow, Nat King Cole, and the Gatlin Brothers. Because of these influences, he is able to sing many styles of music with great expertise. Ronnie's favorite songs are "I Will Lift My Eyes" by Larry Gatlin and "Love Was in the Room" by Mosie Lister. He has also written one song, "In His Time," with Joseph Smith.

The Booth Brothers were named the 1999 SGMA New Artist of the Year, the 2002 SGMA Trio of the Year, and the 2004 Southern Gospel News Male Group of the Year.

Ronnie truly believes God blessed him with the ability to sing and that this talent should be used to serve the Lord. He feels it is his obligation through his singing and testimony to do his best to point people to Christ. "God has allowed me to live my dream of singing, and I want to do everything I can to encourage the saints and point them to the love of God."

Ronnie lives in Plant City, Florida, and has two sons, Ronnie Lee and Daniel.

—*Bob Crichton*

Kelly Crabb Bowling

March 17, 1978—

And let us not be weary in well doing: for in due season we shall reap, if we faint not. Galatians 6:9

he middle daughter of six siblings, Kelly Layne Crabb was born in Owensboro, Kentucky. Kelly sang her first song in church at the age of three and knew in her heart that she wanted to spend her life singing. When she was saved as a teenager, Kelly knew that she wanted to sing only Christian music. Kelly's parents were her greatest influences on both her singing and her listening to Christian music.

When the Crabb Family ministry began, Kelly's desire to serve the Lord through music was fulfilled. Kelly is featured on several of the Crabb Family's fifteen number-one songs including "Don't You Wanna Go," "Trail of Tears," and "Jesus Will Do What You Can't."

Kelly is married to Christian music soloist, Mike Bowling. He has recorded such hits as "Thank God for the Preacher," "The Call," "Take Him Back," and many others. Kelly and Mike have two daughters, Loryn Hope and Katelanne Elaine.

Kelly has been influenced not only by her parents but also by such artists as the Hoppers, the Isaacs, the Goodmans, the Hinsons, the McGruders, and Michael English. Like her siblings, Kelly has many favorite songs, but the most treasured is "Holy Ground." The Isaacs sang this song at Kelly and Mike's wedding.

"Don't You Wanna Go," featuring Kelly, won the Crabb Family its first Dove Award for Southern Gospel Song of the Year in 2003. "Don't You Wanna Go" was the first single from *A Crabb Collection*, winner of the 2003 Dove Award for Southern Gospel Album of the Year.

—Allison Stinson

Mike Bowling

July 13, 1965—

Trust in the LORD with all thine heart; and lean not unto thine own understanding. In all thy ways acknowledge him, and he shall direct thy paths. Proverbs 3:5–6

ichael Lorhen Bowling was born in London, Kentucky. At a young age, Mike and everyone who knew him sensed a special calling on his life. At nine, Mike began playing piano and singing in church. At fourteen, he began traveling with his aunt and uncle, the Mullins Family, on weekends. When Mike was only sixteen years old, a lifelong dream was fulfilled. He was offered a job with the legendary Le Fevres and moved to Atlanta, Georgia. After a few years, Mike returned home and formed a group with his brother and cousins. He also completed a degree in respiratory therapy.

In 1995 Mike began singing with the New Hinsons, and in October he joined the Perrys. He was featured on their first number-one song, "Not Even a Stone," written by Gerald Crabb. While Mike was with the Perrys, he met his future wife, Kelly, of the Crabb Family, at a concert in Boaz, Alabama. Even after their marriage on April 6, 1998, Mike and Kelly remained with their respective groups. In 1999 when they learned they were expecting their first child, they decided the time apart was too much; and Mike began his solo career, which has grown beyond his greatest expectations.

In addition to singing as a soloist at all of the Crabb Family appearances, Mike played piano for the group. He now travels exclusively as a solo artist singing on as many of the Crabb Family's dates as possible. Mike is a talented songwriter, writing much of his own material. He has several number-one songs to his credit.

Mike and Kelly have two daughters, Loryn Hope and Katelanne Elaine. Mike's greatest influences in life are his parents and grandparents. His musical influences include Alphus Le Fevre and the late Kenny Hinson. "Please Forgive Me" by Gerald Crabb is Mike's favorite song.

—Allison Stinson

John Bowman

September 15, 1970—

Then remembered I the word of the Lord, how that he said, John indeed baptized with water; but ye shall be baptized with the Holy Ghost. Forasmuch then as God gave them the like gift as he did unto us, who believed on the Lord Jesus Christ; what was I, that I could withstand God? When they heard these things, they held their peace, and glorified God, saying, Then hath God also to the Gentiles granted repentance unto life. Acts 11:16–18

J ohn Bowman grew up in Ararat, Virginia, with his sister, Rachel. As the son of Bobby and Diane Bowman, he learned to play many different instruments when he was quite young. As the husband of Rebecca Isaacs Bowman, John is a current member of the family group, the Isaacs. He is an excellent multi-instrumentalist who has worked and traveled with Alison Krauss and Union Station as well as Doyle Lawson and Quicksilver.

The Isaacs have traveled as a group for over 30 years and are based in LaFollette, Tennessee. Their unique style blends bluegrass harmonies and instrumentation with modern southern gospel lyrics. The group's musical influences come from all genres of music, including bluegrass, rhythm and blues, folk, contemporary acoustic, and southern gospel. The Isaacs perform frequently at the Grand Ole Opry and are active members of the Gaither Homecoming Video and Concert Series. They travel throughout the year performing nationally. The Isaacs have been asked to perform the National Anthem for many events, including a Cincinnati Bengals football game, several Nashville Predators hockey games, various political rallies, and recently at Carnegie Hall for a Gaither Homecoming video.

In 1997 John was called into the ministry. When not on tour with the Isaacs, he holds revivals. John and Rebecca have two children, Levi Payton and Jakobi Seren.

John's favorite song is "Stand Still," written by his wife.

Rebecca Isaacs Bowman

August 2, 1975—

When thou passest through the waters, I will be with thee; and through the rivers, they shall not overflow thee: when thou walkest through the fire, thou shalt not be burned; neither shall the flame kindle upon thee. Isaiah 43:2

Youngest daughter of the acclaimed family group, the Isaacs, Rebecca Isaacs Bowman has recorded more than twenty albums and made thousands of live appearances. She is an award-winning songwriter who has made guest appearances as a vocalist with Dolly Parton, Bryan Sutton, Paul Simon, Ralph Stanley, and Mark Lowry. Her grandmother, Fay Fishman, along with Tony Rice, James Taylor, the Marshall Family, and Dolly Parton, influenced Rebecca musically. Rebecca's repertoire of written songs includes "Stand Still," "Friend to the End," and "He Understood My Tears."

While they are best known as a family act, the individual accomplishments of the Isaacs could have made stars of any of them. In their early days, the children appeared on their parents' regular local cable-access television show. In 1986 they became a family band, bought a bus, and took their music on the road. At one time, a promoter told the group that they could forget about being accepted in the southern gospel world unless they changed their style. They rejected his advice because they loved their music and were comfortable with their style. That decision proved to make all the difference in the world.

Rebecca married John Bowman on June 4, 1994. They have two children, Levi Payton and Jakobi Seren.

Rebecca's favorite song is "The Good Shepherd."

Jim Brady

May 19, 1970—

He that dwelleth in the secret place of the most High shall abide under the shadow of the Almighty. I will say of the LORD, He is my refuge and my fortress: my God; in him will I trust. Psalm 91:1–2

ames David Brady, the baritone singer with the Booth Brothers, has a long history of music and singing. He began singing with his mom, dad, and seven brothers and sisters when he was five years old. They called themselves the Brady Family but were affectionately known as the Christian Brady Bunch. He was reared in Houston, Texas, and subsequently moved to Ohio.

Jim remembers as a kid always hiding a copy of the *Singing News* in his schoolbooks so that he could keep up on the latest gospel music news. This keen interest made him a trivia expert on artists, songs, and writers. When Jim was sixteen, he started writing songs and has since written over one hundred songs. Such artists as Ivan Parker, the Ruppes, and Lordsong have recorded some of his songs.

Jim met Melissa at a gospel concert in Atlanta, Georgia. For nine years, he sang with the Shulers, a trio composed of Jack Shuler, Melissa Shuler Brady, and Jim. The trio was best known for their enjoyable mix of traditional and progressive southern gospel. Jim liked to call what they sang "new southern." The Shulers were nominated for Horizon Group of the Year in the 1997 *Singing News* Fan Awards, and they were nominated for the SGMA New Artist Award in 1999.

Melissa is a talented songwriter and singer in her own right. She and Jim have also co-written many songs, including an album, *Our Love Songs*, which has a bit of a "pop" feel.

The main objective Jim and Melissa want people to know is, "What we do is always and only about the Lord and telling others about Him. When we write and when we sing, it is our desire and our goal, first and foremost, to lift Him up in praise." Jim's favorite song is "He's Been Faithful" by Carol Cymbala. His favorite singer is his wife, Melissa.

When they're not on the road, Jim and Melissa live in Nashville, Tennessee.

—Bob Crichton

Anthony Burger

June 5, 1961—

And we know that all things work together for good to them that love God, to them who are the called according to his purpose. Romans 8:28

A nthony Burger is a native of Cleveland, Tennessee. Even though he is a man with much to say, he does very little talking. His music speaks volumes, however. Anthony's piano playing is a miracle. When he was a little boy he burned both hands, and the doctor told him he would never use them again.

Anthony can barely remember a moment when he wasn't playing the piano. He is the youngest student ever accepted into the University of Tennessee's Cadek Conservatory of Music in Chattanooga. Anthony's years at Cadek exposed him to many forms of music, including the classics. However, after dedicating his life to Christ at the age of nine, gospel music became his favorite.

As a teen, Anthony joined the Kingsmen, and at seventeen he was nominated as one of southern gospel music's Top Five Musicians by *Singing News*. He held the title for ten years. His music has garnered much acclaim resulting in more than fifteen awards and nominations, including Dove Awards, Fan Awards, Diamond Awards, and the SGMA's Musician of the Year Award.

In the mid-1990s the Gaither Vocal Band invited Anthony, after he had set out on a solo career, on their Homecoming Tour. He regularly travels with Mark Lowry.

Whether he's performing at New York City's Beacon Theater, the White House, the Kennedy Center, a Billy Graham Crusade, a Gaither Homecoming Concert, or traveling across international borders to Canada, Ireland, Scotland, England, or the Caribbean, Anthony thanks God for using his talent to bless and encourage.

He and his wife, LuAnn, have two sons and a daughter.

Candy Hemphill Christmas

June 10, 1961—

Therefore I say unto you, What things soever ye desire, when ye pray, believe that ye receive them, and ye shall have them. Mark 11:24

orn in Bastrop, Louisiana, Candy's roots in gospel music go back three generations. Her grandmother was a member of the Goodman family and her parents, Joel and LaBreeska, met when Joel was playing guitar at a service where LaBreeska and the Goodman family were singing. Named Carmel Lynn but nicknamed Candy soon after her birth, she was born just two weeks after her father had taken a pastorate in Bastrop.

In the early 1970s the family moved to Nashville, Tennessee, to explore opportunities in the Christian concert and recording industry. Candy and her brothers, Joey and Trent, enrolled in correspondence courses and joined their parents on the road. In 1973 when she was only thirteen, Candy's first recording, "I Came on Business for the King," reached fifth place on the gospel music charts.

Candy chose to put her solo career on hold when she met and married Kent Christmas, a dynamic young evangelist. She felt her young family needed a normal and secure life, not caught up in the confusion of separate road careers. Daughter Jasmine was born in 1988. In 1994 son Nicholas arrived three months early and spent nine weeks in the hospital. The young family had no insurance and no income during that time. People they had met all across the country heard of their need and sent help—their medical bill of more than three-quarters of a million dollars was paid.

Candy's career has recently taken a new direction. She is recording once again, creating her own songs, and collaborating with others.

Kelly Nelon Clark

December 1, 1959—

For I know the thoughts that I think toward you, saith the LORD, thoughts of peace, and not of evil, to give you an expected end. Jeremiah 29:11

elly has been in professional Christian music for twenty-seven years. Touring the world presenting the gospel in song has been her life's calling since she was thirteen years old. Her father, Rex Nelon, is a gospel music legend who passed to his daughter a legacy of excellence and commitment to the cause of Christ.

Kelly's voice has been heard from small country churches to Carnegie Hall and every venue in between. Kelly continues to set the standard female vocalists follow. She tours on selected dates with her family group, the Nelons, along with her husband and two daughters. Kelly also serves on the staff of their home church in Powder Springs, Georgia.

Every note of every song that she sings reflects Kelly's endless pursuit of training and knowledge. In addition to her work with the Nelons, Kelly has recorded six solo projects. Music fans and peers have recognized Kelly's hard work, dedication, and talent with three Grammy nominations and six Dove Awards. *Singing News* readers have selected Kelly as Alto of the Year four times and Female Artist of the Year four times. The readers of *Voice Magazine* selected Kelly as Female Artist of the Year three times.

"My father took great pride in developing new talent. Because he was grateful for the opportunities given him when he started, he never missed the chance to do the same for someone who had talent and possessed a love and desire to perform gospel music—including me," Kelly shares.

—Jason Clark

Cynthia Clawson

October 11, 1948—

Jesus wept. John 11:35

ynthia was born in Houston, Texas, and has been singing the gospel for more than four decades. *Billboard Magazine* called her the woman with "the most awesome voice in gospel music." She has received a Grammy and five Dove Awards for her work.

Cynthia was three years old when her father first asked her to sing in the small church he pastored. She has not stopped singing since—from local neighborhood churches to Robert Schuller's televised "Hour of Power" to appearing in London's Wembley Stadium.

A graduate of Howard Payne University with a major in vocal performance and a minor in piano, Cynthia was also awarded an honorary degree—doctor of humane letters—from Houston Baptist University in 1995. During her senior year in college, Cynthia was spotted by a CBS television producer who signed her to headline a summer replacement for "The Carol Burnett Show." That engagement led to a recording contract with Buryl Red, who was writing a musical with friend Ragan Courtney. Cynthia was invited to record the solos for the original cast album. There Cynthia and Ragan met, married within six months, and began a lifetime of creative collaboration.

Throughout her career, Cynthia has continued to push beyond the boundaries of traditional gospel music. Her rendition of "Softly and Tenderly" set the evocative tone for the soundtrack of the Academy Award-winning movie, *The Trip to Bountiful.*

Currently, Cynthia and Ragan are co-pastors of Tarrytown Baptist Church in Austin, Texas. Son Will is pursuing a recording career in Los Angeles, and daughter Lily is a religious studies major at the University of Texas at Austin.

—Laurie Winton

Aaron Crabb

November 27, 1979—

Now faith is the substance of things hoped for, the evidence of things not seen. Hebrews 11:1

orn in Owensboro, Kentucky, David Aaron Crabb is the youngest, by only a few minutes, of the six Crabb siblings. His twin brother, Adam, came into the world just before him. Aaron, who sings and plays acoustic guitar with the Crabb Family, actually began his onstage career by playing the bass guitar. Aaron's parents, his sister, Kelly, and his brother, Jason, had been traveling for several months when Aaron was born.

Aaron was always very active in sports and enjoyed attending public school. During a summer vacation he traveled with his family to a concert where the Goodmans and Phil Cross & Poet Voices were on the program. Aaron had developed an interest in playing the bass and in that concert joined the family for the first time. He knew immediately that he had found his place.

After his parents retired from the road, Aaron stepped up to the front line of singing. He also answered the call to preach and followed in the footsteps of his father, Gerald Crabb, as a songwriter. He has written several songs that his family has recorded and has co-written songs with his brother-in-law, Mike Bowling.

Aaron's greatest influences have been his family and such other artists as Michael English, Russ Taff, and the Gaither Vocal Band. His favorite song is "Through the Fire," written by his father and sung by the Crabb Family at the 2002 Dove Awards program. One of Aaron's career highlights is the Crabb Family's 2003 Grammy nomination.

Aaron and his wife, Amanda, have one son, Elijah David.

—Allison Stinson

Adam Crabb

For we wrestle not against flesh and blood, but against principalities, against powers, against the rulers of the darkness of this world, against spiritual wickedness in high places. Ephesians 6:12

dam Lee, the middle son of the six Crabb children, was born a few minutes before his twin brother, Aaron, in Owensboro, Kentucky. Adam sings and plays harmonica with the Crabb Family. He was the last of the six siblings to join the family ministry full time. Although Adam was reluctant, he knew in his heart all along that God had called him. Adam recalls sitting in church one night and feeling God deal with his heart to step out and minister.

Adam's father, Gerald Crabb, is his greatest influence. Gerald, a six-time GMA award-winning songwriter, bought Adam's first harmonica at a Cracker Barrel restaurant. Some of his favorite singers and musicians, including Michael English and Terry McMillan, have also influenced him. Adam's favorite song is one his father wrote called "The Healer."

Adam is blessed with a God-given talent to play music, and he serves God with 100 percent of his ability and his heart. He sings much of the group's harmony.

Featuring Adam, the Crabb Family's project, *The Walk*, was awarded the 2003 Dove Award for Southern Gospel Album of the Year. Adam has received numerous award nominations for young artists and musicians. He is one of the most talented musicians in Christian music today.

Adam and his wife, Kristi, have a daughter, Hannah Grace.

—Allison Stinson

Gerald Crabb

January 2, 1958—

Blessed is the man that walketh not in the counsel of the ungodly, nor standeth in the way of sinners, nor sitteth in the seat of the scornful. But his delight is in the law of the LORD . . . and whatsoever he doeth shall prosper. Psalm 1:1–3

Gerald Douglas Crabb was born in the tiny community of Rosine, Kentucky. He was the only boy in a family of four sisters. As young children, Gerald and his sisters often "played church." Gerald's sisters say that he always landed the role of the preacher. What they did not know was that God had begun an awesome work in the life of the small boy. Gerald's life revolves around playing music, singing, writing songs, preaching, and pastoring.

While pastoring a church in Philpot, Kentucky, Gerald felt God leading him to launch a music ministry with his children. As he saw each of his children developing his or her unique talents, he knew that it was time to move forward with the ministry of the Crabb Family.

Gerald Crabb's story is one of humble, modest beginnings and hardships. Gerald has a powerful testimony of a battle with and deliverance from an alcohol addiction. He has taken the hard knocks in life and turned them into melodies. He has allowed the Lord to transfer times of brokenness and heartache into hope and joy.

Gerald has been named GMA's spotlight Songwriter of the Year seven times in the southern gospel division. He also shared BMI's highest honor, Gospel Songwriter of the Year, with Steven Curtis Chapman. The Crabb Family's album, *The Walk*, featuring songs written by Gerald, was nominated for a Grammy. Although his songs are listed among many of his peers' favorites, one of Gerald's favorite songs, "I Still Trust You," was written by James McFall and is the motto of his life.

In 2002 Gerald retired from the road. He remains very active in his children's ministry while focusing more on his personal ministry of preaching, singing, and writing.

—Allison Stinson

Jason Crabb

March 3, 1977—

Jesus saith unto her, Mary. She turned herself, and saith unto him, Rabboni; which is to say, Master. John 20:16

J ason Douglas Crabb was born in Owensboro, Kentucky. As the eldest of six, Jason always looked up to his father, Gerald Crabb, and followed in his footsteps both as a singer and as a preacher. Even as a young child, Jason knew he would somehow be involved in music and in ministry. He began singing and playing various instruments at an early age. Jason developed his talent by singing and playing in church and was ready to step out into full-time ministry as soon as he felt the calling of God on his life.

Jason is featured on many of the Crabb Family hits: "Please Forgive Me," "Through the Fire," "The Lamb, the Lion, and the King," "Still Holdin' On," "Sure Miss You," "Please Come Down to Me," "That's No Mountain," and "The Cross," all written by his father. Jason helped his father write Mike Bowling's number-one hit, "Thank God for the Preacher."

Jason and his wife, Shellye, have a daughter, Ashleigh Taylor. Jason and Gerald co-wrote a song for Ashleigh called "Forever," that has become Jason's favorite song. He recalls that the song, "I Still Trust You," has been an encouragement many times in his life. Jason's greatest influence has been his father, as well as Michael English, Russ Taff, the Gaither Vocal Band, and many other artists in Christian music.

"The Cross," which features Jason, won the 2003 Dove Award for Southern Gospel Song of the Year. *Singing News* fans named Jason Favorite Young Artist in 2001. He has received numerous other awards and nominations as a male vocalist.

—Allison Stinson

Kathy Crabb

February 11, 1956—

*For I know the thoughts that I think toward you, saith the LORD,
thoughts of peace, and not of evil, to give you an expected end.*
Jeremiah 29:11

athy Jo Coppage was born in Centertown, Kentucky. No one
knew at that time just what God had in store for the life of
this new baby girl. Kathy is the youngest of four children
(two sisters and a brother). At a very young age she demonstrated sharp business skills and a strong work ethic. Although the Crabb
Family members often walk onto stages to accept awards or receive honors,
Kathy Crabb is the unmentioned secret to the success of the Crabb
Family.

Kathy has six children: Krystal, Jason, Kelly, Adam, Aaron, and Terah,
plus eight grandchildren. The Lord placed in Kathy's heart the desire
to embark upon a music ministry with her children.

While living in Philpot, Kentucky, Kathy spent countless hours with
her children gathered around a piano. She helped each to develop his
or her musical and vocal abilities and taught them to sing harmony. Kathy
still relies on the direction of God daily to lead her children in their
ministry. At one time or another she has served as a role model to nearly
every singer, songwriter, musician, or businessperson in the southern
gospel music industry.

Kathy believes in hard work and teaches her family the same values
that she lives. The results are evident through her children's number-
one songs, Dove Awards, and Grammy nomination, not to mention their
efforts with spreading the gospel and changing lives. Kathy's favorite
song is one that her children recorded, "He'll Make a Way."

Kathy's desire is to manage her children's ministry faithfully and obedi-
ently and to mentor young singers and musicians who are in love with
the music, the message, and most of all, the Lord.   —*Allison Stinson*

Andraé Crouch

Being confident of this very thing, that he which hath begun a good work in you will perform it until the day of Jesus Christ.
Philippians 1:6

ndraé Crouch and his twin sister, Sandra, began their music careers in their father's church in the San Fernando Valley in California. They had no formal training. At fourteen, Andraé wrote one of gospel music's classic songs, "The Blood Will Never Lose Its Power." At the time, he thought it wasn't good and threw it away. Sandra knew better and retrieved it.

While attending Valley Junior College in California, Andraé felt the call to ministry and in 1965 formed the Disciples with Perry Morgan and Billy Thedford.

Songwriter Audrey Mieir, whom Andraé affectionately called his "great white mama," introduced him to her publishers, Tim and Hal Spencer, at Manna Music. Ralph Carmichael recorded Andraé Crouch and the Disciples on Light Records. Their first album, *Take the Message Everywhere*, was released in 1968. In the early days they were invited to sing at the National Quartet Convention in Nashville and were a big hit.

Crossing every boundary, Andraé's music has been recorded by Elvis Presley, Quincy Jones, Madonna, and countless other singers and groups. Andraé has written hundreds of songs including "My Tribute (To God Be the Glory)," "Through It All," "The Broken Vessel," and "Soon and Very Soon." His movie score credits include *The Lion King* and *Free Willy*. He even has a star on the Hollywood Walk of Fame. CeCe Winans has credited Andraé's music as "one of the most important influences on me and my family."

A favorite moment in the Gaither Homecoming Series occurred when CeCe Winans and Michael W. Smith sang Andraé Crouch's songs on the Billy Graham video. In 1997 Andraé was inducted into the GMA Gospel Music Hall of Fame as an individual on the same night Andraé Crouch and the Disciples were inducted as a group.

Andraé and his sister, Sandra, continue to have a close relationship. Today they are co-pastors of the church where their father was pastor.

—Judy Spencer Nelon

Denver Crumpler

August 17, 1912—March 21, 1957

For God sent not his Son into the world to condemn the world; but that the world through him might be saved. John 3:17

Denver Dale Crumpler was born in Village, Arkansas, near Magnolia. As a child Denver sang in churches and at all-day singings near his home. As radio became the norm in many homes, the public began to hear his wonderful Irish tenor voice.

Shreveport, Louisiana, became Denver's home and then Little Rock, Arkansas, where he joined the Stamps-Melody Boys in the mid-1930s. He learned to play the guitar as a young man accompanying the group. The Rangers Quartet gained respect when Denver joined their group in 1938. For several years the Rangers made their home in Charlotte, North Carolina, where they worked with a local radio station.

Doy Ott had sung with the Rangers but later joined the Statesmen Quartet. He persuaded Denver to join the Statesmen at about the same time they became one of the most popular singing groups in the nation. The Statesmen were asked to sing the title song for the movie, *A Man Called Peter.* They later traveled to New York to sing the song for the film's premiere. The Statesmen Quartet was declared the winner on a nationally televised "Arthur Godfrey's Talent Scouts" program. This exposure increased their traveling as they toured from Texas to the east coast.

Denver's faith grew stronger during his last days. He settled in Decatur, Georgia, with his family and became very active in his church. Even when he was traveling with the quartets, he would always try to make it back home for church on Sunday.

Jessy Dixon

*Fear thou not; for I am with thee: be not dismayed; for I am thy
God: I will strengthen thee; yea, I will help thee; yea, I will uphold
thee with the right hand of my righteousness.* Isaiah 41:10

essy Dixon's résumé reads like a combined Who's Who in gospel
music and a worldwide travelogue. This man has been "on the
move" since his first public performance when he was five.

James Cleveland, the first of many gospel greats to record
Jessy's compositions, discovered Jessy not long after his first public performance. Over the years Jessy has written hundreds of songs and performed with such folks as Diana Ross, Natalie Cole, Mahalia Jackson,
Cher, Bette Midler, James Taylor, and Al Greene. He has gone on world
tours with Paul Simon.

In addition to his international smash hit song, "I Am Redeemed,"
three gold records, and multiple Grammy Award nominations, his friend
and gospel music producer, Bob MacKenzie, invited him—no, coerced
him—to a Homecoming recording session at the Gaither Studios. Though
Jessy knew the Gaithers' songs and reputation, he was hesitant to just
drop in on this session where he expected to be out of his comfort zone.
What was this crazy MacKenzie man getting him into? Just a huge chunk
of the rest of his life!

Following the session break, during which Jessy "just sat, smiled,
and sang along with the familiar tunes," he returned to the studio and
found a handful of the artists singing "Highway to Heaven," just for
fun. As the Homecoming group reassembled, Jessy became Jessy! He
quietly began to teach the group seated around him a new counter-
melody. It caught on, and as more and more singers arrived, it became
a real jam session.

Enter Bill Gaither, famous for recognizing a great moment, who
commanded, "Roll the cameras!" For at least fifteen minutes, this
gathering of Homecoming Friends found themselves on an up-tempo
journey with a new friend. Jessy had a new family, and Homecoming
Concerts have never been the same!

—*Joy MacKenzie*

61

Sue Dodge

December 20, 1949—

For I know the thoughts that I think toward you, saith the LORD, thoughts of peace, and not of evil, to give you an expected end. Jeremiah 29:11

Sue Chenault was born in Little Rock, Arkansas, and can easily trace her gospel roots back to her childhood home and parents who nurtured her love of music. They purchased a piano for her and encouraged her to sing. By the age of fourteen, she began her professional singing career with the T. O. Miller Trio.

Not long after she won "Miss Congeniality" in the 1968 Miss Arkansas beauty pageant, Sue successfully auditioned with the Downings, a new group in gospel music who immediately became one of its finest. She went on to sing soprano for the Speer Family for four years until her marriage to Amos Dodge in 1974.

One of Sue's special memories is performing a patriotic medley prior to a speech by President Reagan. One of the selections, "God Bless the USA," was the president's favorite. Moments after she sang, he opened his remarks by saying, "Politicians are rarely rendered speechless, but you'll have to excuse me. Young Lady, that was wonderful."

With a musical career spanning three decades and having won four consecutive Dove Awards for Female Vocalist, Sue is certainly a voice to be reckoned with! She was honored as a former member of the Speer Family when the group was inducted into the GMA Gospel Music Hall of Fame.

Sue continues to travel full time, sharing in churches and on television, and singing and speaking at conferences. She also sings, plays the piano, and participates in pastoral ministry with husband Amos in McLean, Virginia.

Daughter Tara and her husband, Travis Goodman, grandson of gospel legends Howard and Vestal Goodman, have made her the grandmother of Sydney Elizabeth and Madeline Grace.   —*Laurie Winton*

Ann Downing

June 12, 1945—

I had fainted, unless I had believed to see the goodness of the LORD in the land of the living. Psalm 27:13

orn Virginia Ann Sanders in Pittsboro, Mississippi, Ann Downing grew up on her family's cotton farm dreaming of the day when she would sing gospel music all over the world. Her family made sure she had opportunities to realize that dream by connecting her with the best music teachers and singing schools in the area. Ann listened to a variety of music, including Patti Page and Rosemary Clooney, but it was her interest in Ginger Smith Laxson, soprano for the Speers, that really paid off. Right out of high school, Ann was offered a job with the Speer Family, impressing them by knowing all their songs. Ann quickly became one of the most popular vocalists in gospel music with her signature songs, "I Must Tell Jesus" and "On the Sunny Banks."

Within a year of forming the Downings with husband Paul, Ann earned the Dove Award for Female Vocalist, and three years later *Singing News* named her Queen of Gospel Music. The Downings changed the face of gospel music with such songs as "Operator," "I've Got Confidence," and "Greater Is He That Is in Me," yet they continued to appeal to traditionalists with "Caught Up Together" and "I'll Soon Be Gone." Garnering eighteen top-twenty songs in a seven-year period, the Downings are notably one of gospel music's legendary groups.

Continuing in full-time ministry since Paul's death in 1992 and encouraging others in their journey, Ann shares her intensely personal story of a God faithful through great joy and great loss. Ann celebrates over forty years in music and ministry. She was inducted into the Hall of Fame as a member with the Speer Family. —*Laurie Winton*

Paul Downing

December 2, 1932—February 23, 1992

*How precious also are thy thoughts unto me, O God! how great is
the sum of them!* Psalm 139:17

P aul Shirley Downing, Jr. was born in Manila, Arkansas, the
eldest of four children. Paul spent his childhood years in
Tupelo, Mississippi, before joining the Navy in 1948. Ever
charming, he enjoyed a successful career in sales before
finding his home in gospel music. Vocal coach and encourager, Leroy
Abernathy, took an interest in Paul's deep bass voice, comparing it to
one of the best bass singers from the 1940s, Aycel (A. D.) Sowards.
Paul sang with Abernathy's All Stars Quartet, as well as the Rangers
Quartet and the Dixie Echoes. He loved Bill Lyles' singing and
dreamed of the day he could sing with the Blackwood Brothers.

However, a pretty gal from Mississippi who was singing with the
Speer Family at the time won his heart and changed those dreams.
Paul met and married Ann Sanders in 1968, and within a year they
formed the Downings, which became one of the most popular groups
of the 1970s. Known for introducing many songs to gospel music, including "Rise and Be Healed," "I've Got Confidence," and "Greater
Is He That Is in Me," the Downings enjoyed eighteen top-twenty
songs in seven years. Paul's unforgettable smile and ability to share his
heart in a very special way won the hearts of fans. In 1973 he won the
Singing News Fan Award for Favorite Bass.

Through much prayer and healing, Paul and Ann rebuilt their falter-
ing marriage in the late 1980s and began reaching out to other couples
and hurting kids in need of emotional healing. Paul passed away February 23, 1992, with his dear Ann by his side. It is a little known fact
that Paul vocalized the last note on the piano in a vocal lesson shortly
before his death. He leaves behind a rich ministry legacy of sincerely
reaching out to the unloved and to hurting people who came his way.

—Laurie Winton

Jeff Easter

March 18, 1960—

For God so loved the world, that he gave his only begotten Son, that whosoever believeth in him should not perish, but have everlasting life. John 3:16

orn Amos Jeffrey Easter, Jeff Easter began playing bass with his family, the Easter Brothers, at the age of eleven. Jeff's daddy was his biggest musical influence. Singing with his family, Jeff developed the bluegrass-tinged voice and country pickin' that he uses today.

Jeff met Sheri Williamson of the Lewis Family at an Albert E. Brumley Sundown to Sunup Gospel Singing in Arkansas. He was playing bass for the Singing Americans. Within a year, Jeff and Sheri were married and formed their own successful trio, Jeff & Sheri Easter. The group has given new meaning to the southern gospel music world as they have added their distinctive touch of country-driven melodies and down-home charm to the gospel message. Sheri's raspy, award-winning vocals joined with Jeff's musicianship, bluegrass-oriented vocals, and stage antics to create a winning combination.

After two Dove Awards, multiple nominations, and Gaither Homecoming Concert Tours and Videos, Jeff & Sheri Easter remain focused on the gospel message and songs about life and love in our everyday world. Their uplifting songs about the relationship between a wife and husband show the importance of love and family.

Jeff describes himself as "the typical preacher's kid" and affirms that all the bad things one hears about preachers' kids are true! For Jeff, his teenage years were filled with bad choices that led to discouragement. He feels that his ministry in Christian music is one of encouragement.

Jeff and Sheri reside in Lincolnton, Georgia, with their two children, Madison and Morgan.

—Celeste Winstead

Sheri Easter

October 27, 1963—

*But they that wait upon the L*ORD *shall renew their strength; they shall mount up with wings as eagles; they shall run, and not be weary; and they shall walk, and not faint.* Isaiah 40:31

orn Sheri Lynn Williamson, Sheri Easter began singing with her family, the legendary Lewis Family, at the age of fifteen. Her mother, Polly Lewis Copsey, who has been her biggest musical influence, has a soulful sound that Sheri loves.

Sheri married Jeff Easter, known previously for his singing and musicianship with the Easter Brothers; not long afterward, the two formed their own family group that has been traveling for over fifteen years. Jeff & Sheri Easter are known for such hits as "Roses Will Bloom Again," "Thread of Hope," "Praise His Name" and many others.

Sheri has been named Female Vocalist of the Year four times and Alto of the Year eight times. The group has received a Grammy nomination and two Dove Awards for Country Album of the Year and Country Recorded Song of the Year. It is known for its unique country, bluegrass, gospel style and for singing not only gospel songs about heaven but also songs about everyday life and love.

Making their home in Lincolnton, Georgia, Jeff and Sheri have two children, Madison and Morgan, who now travel and perform with the group. Sheri stays busy as a wife, mother, and group business manager. She also enjoys managing her clothing boutique, The Easter Parade, as well as writing songs.

While she was growing up, Sheri's family was always a close one. Therefore, when her father passed away suddenly from a heart attack when she was twenty, her life was devastated. Perhaps that has been an influence on her calling to minister through music: "My ministry is one of compassion and empathy and encouraging people who are hurting."

—*Celeste Winstead*

Michael English

April 12, 1962—

For God hath not given us the spirit of fear; but of power, and of love, and of a sound mind. 2 Timothy 1:7

orn in North Carolina, Michael was reared in a strict, religious family. He was still in grade school when he began singing with his family's group, the Singing Samaritans. In 1980 he joined the Singing Americans and then sang with the Happy Goodman Family. Michael joined the Couriers for a short time and then returned to the Singing Americans for a year. His big break came when Bill Gaither invited him to join the Gaither Vocal Band in 1984.

Michael's first solo album, which was released in 1992, included the landmark songs, "In Christ Alone," "Mary, Did You Know?" "Solid as the Rock," and "Heaven." His next album, *Hope*, included "Message of Mercy," "Love Moves in Mysterious Ways," and "Holding out Hope to You."

In 1995 Michael released a pop album with Wynonna. In 1996 "Your Love Amazes Me" from his pop album *Freedom* became a Top-Ten hit on Adult-Contemporary charts. Three years later, he returned to his roots with an album simply called *Gospel*.

The next major release, *Heaven to Earth*, was in 2000. While premiering it on the Trinity Broadcast Network, Michael gave his testimony about how God had helped him through the pain in his life, his struggle with addiction to painkillers, and his rehab experiences.

Michael married Marcie Stambaugh in 2002. They have a daughter named Isabella Grace. Michael also has a daughter, Megan Leigh Ann English, from a previous marriage. She has a beautiful voice and occasionally sings with her dad.

Michael has reconnected with his old friends, Mark Lowry and Reggie Smith, and they are considering a project together.

Larry Ford

November 10, 1947—

Let the word of Christ dwell in you richly in all wisdom; teaching and admonishing one another in psalms and hymns and spiritual songs, singing with grace in your hearts to the Lord. Colossians 3:16

 arry Don Ford is originally from Lubbock, Texas. His music ministry has taken him to forty-eight of the fifty states. Larry's facility with language has made it possible for him to carry the message of Christ to twenty-seven foreign countries. From the sounds of grand opera to the stages of southern gospel, Larry has found audiences responding to his commanding voice and anointed ministry.

Larry began traveling and singing across Texas when he was sixteen. Lou Wills Hildreth produced Larry's first recording that same year. Larry left music for a couple of years but returned as a featured soloist with Paul and Ann Downing's group. In 1980 he became a part of the James Blackwood Quartet, singing tenor for the group on a temporary basis.

Larry's early gospel music influences were his beloved friend and mentor, James Blackwood and the Blackwood Quartet, as well as the Couriers and the Imperials. Among classical musicians, he loved listening to Placido Domingo and Jussi Bjoerling. Today Larry's favorite classical tenor is his brother, Bruce.

In February 2003 Larry was awarded a Grammy for Best Southern Gospel Recording for *They Called Him Mr. Gospel Music: A Tribute to James Blackwood.* Larry participated in Bill and Gloria Gaither's Grammy Award winner, *Homecoming at the Kennedy Center* in 2000. He has been a featured soloist on many of the Gaither Homecoming videos.

Larry and his wife, Sherryl, were married in 1970. They have five sons, one daughter, and four grandchildren.

Scott Fowler

July 9, 1966—

For I know the thoughts that I think toward you, saith the LORD, thoughts of peace, and not of evil, to give you an expected end.
Jeremiah 29:11

aving been a fan of quartet music since he was sixteen, Scott was asked in 1991 to join his favorite group, the Cathedrals. He quickly became one of the most popular baritones in the field of southern gospel music. His dynamic voice and winning personality made him a favorite.

Scott says the greatest influences on his life and ministry were his dad and Grandpa Hamm. He also stated, "Both men were great preachers, but beyond that they were mentors and heroes. All of my favorite memories seem to have both of these men present. They are in heaven today, but the contributions they left me and my life will remain here forever." Scott's earliest memories are of singing in church. His favorite song is "Wonderful Grace of Jesus."

When in 1999 the Cathedrals Quartet said farewell, Scott and Roger Bennett formed one of today's most popular quartets, Legacy Five. Scott sings lead while Glenn Dustin, Frank Seamans, and Scott Howard complete the other three parts. Roger Bennett rounds out the group on piano and occasionally sings.

In 2004 Scott was honored with the SGMG Humanitarian Award for his efforts during friend and Legacy Five co-founder Roger Bennett's battle with cancer. Scott was the driving force behind raising the money for Roger's bone marrow transplant, as well as other expenses accrued during his illness.

Scott Fowler is married to Taryn Davis, daughter of Christian comedian, Ken Davis. "Taryn grew up in a home where the husband traveled on weekends, so she was accustomed to the life-style." They have a son, Preston, and live in Franklin, Tennessee. —*Crystal Burchette*

Bill Gaither

March 28, 1936—

And ye shall know the truth, and the truth shall make you free.
John 8:32

Just out of college and teaching high-school English, Bill Gaither took on a part-time job as choir director at his home church. That's when he first wondered if there might be a need in the church for songs that combined good theology with the stories of everyday struggles. As history would show, Bill and his co-writer (his wife Gloria) would fill that void with nearly 700 songs, pioneering a new genre often referred to as "Inspirational."

In many ways, as much as he is a concert artist, songwriter, video producer, mentor, and entrepreneur, Bill Gaither is still, in his heart of hearts, a choir director. And for the last decade, he's had the opportunity to direct some of the top voices in the country as they've traversed the world—including stops in Ireland, England, Australia, and Israel—as the Homecoming Friends. With these same "Friends," he produced a succession of nearly one hundred videos, a catalog of videos that gave new life to southern gospel music and its living legends as the twentieth century ended.

In the first years of the twenty-first century Bill continues to release videos that top the *Billboard* video charts, proving that even mainstream audiences are interested in American music that has a message. Appearing on the Homecoming stage each night is Bill's Gaither Vocal Band, a group that when it was born in 1981, redefined the term "quartet." The Vocal Band is one of the first Christian groups to sellout concerts in auditoriums and arenas.

During his thirty-plus years in the business, Bill has gratefully accepted five Grammy Awards and nearly thirty Dove Awards. In 1983 he was inducted into the Gospel Music Association Hall of Fame and in 2000 was honored by the American Society of Composers, Artists, and Publishers as "Christian Songwriter of the Century."

—Jack Williams

Danny Gaither

November 20, 1938—April 6, 2001

Wherefore God also hath highly exalted him, and given him a name which is above every name: That at the name of Jesus every knee should bow, of things in heaven, and things in earth, and things under the earth; And that every tongue should confess that Jesus Christ is Lord, to the glory of God the Father. Philippians 2:9–11

Daniel Joseph Gaither was born and reared in Alexandria, Indiana, the second son of George and Lela Gaither. His foundational role with the Bill Gaither Trio endeared him to audiences around the world. By those who knew him well, Danny is best remembered for the person he was when no one was watching. His timeless, heartfelt vocals propelled the Gaither Trio to critical acclaim, countless awards, and sellout concerts across America.

Danny's first quartet began in his teen years with his brother Bill, cousin Moe, and friend Howard. They called themselves the Log Cabin Four. Upon graduation from Ball State University, Danny sang with the Golden Keys Quartet.

Dan was not only a master musician and solo recording artist, but he was also a skilled carpenter and mechanic. While traveling with his brother, he taught high school and built his first dream home. As a member of the Bill Gaither Trio in 1999, Danny was inducted into the Gospel Music Association Hall of Fame.

A touching moment occurred at a videotaping during Danny's illness when Janet Paschal asked, "Danny, I bet you've come away from all of this with a lot of stuff." Danny replied, "Oh yes, but more importantly, I left a lot of stuff behind. I wouldn't want anyone to go through what I've been through, but having gone through it, I'm far richer." Some years later, Janet was asked to sing a song that she had written, "Another Soldier's Coming Home," at Danny's funeral.

Though a lengthy, courageous battle with cancer cut his life short, Danny will long be remembered for his humanitarian spirit, incredible talent, Christian love, and million-dollar smile.

Danny's favorite hymn to sing was "Oh Love That Will Not Let Me Go." He "Traced the rainbow through the rain" and believed that "Life shall endless be."

—Vonnie Gaither Wright

81

Gloria Gaither

March 4, 1942—

Now unto him that is able to do exceeding abundantly above all that we ask or think, according to the power that worketh in us, Unto him be glory in the church by Christ Jesus throughout all ages, world without end. Amen. Ephesians 3:20–21

 student of French, English, and sociology in college, Gloria Sickal wasn't planning on a career in music. However, she met a determined young songwriter named Bill Gaither. In Bill she found a soulmate who understood her passion for eternal themes beautifully told. Those themes would eventually grace nearly 700 Gaither songs, many of which appear in church hymnals around the world.

Although Gloria performed with the Bill Gaither Trio for twenty years, is heard on sixty Gaither recordings, and can be seen today on music videos with the Homecoming Friends, music is only part of her calling as a communicator. She has written a shelf of books including: *Making Ordinary Days Extraordinary, Creating Family Traditions,* and *What My Parents Did Right.* She has also written a series of children's books. Gloria taught songwriting at the university level, earned a master of arts degree in English literature, has received numerous honorary degrees, and is an active advocate for Christian higher education.

A true bibliophile, Gloria shares her reading recommendations in "Gloria's Book Club," a feature found in each issue of *Homecoming Magazine.* In recent years, she has researched the life and works of American author John Steinbeck. A popular speaker on issues that impact today's Christians, Gloria keeps a keen eye on contemporary culture.

In 2000 the American Society of Composers, Artists, and Publishers recognized Gloria as "Christian Songwriter of the Century" for her musical impact on American culture. But Gloria keeps her accomplishments and commitments in context. Her first priority has always been the making of magical memories for her busy family and encouraging others to do the same for their own families. —*Jack Williams*

Joy Gardner

December 8, 1951—

And the peace of God, which passeth all understanding, shall keep your hearts and minds through Christ Jesus. Philippians 4:7

J oy Dyson was born in Little Rock, Arkansas, into a musical family that considered ministry a priority and embedded in Joy's heart the belief that music can make an eternal difference in the lives of people. Growing up and traveling to all-night singings to hear the Statesmen, the Blackwood Brothers, and the Speer Family fueled her appreciation of gospel music; and in 1970 Joy successfully auditioned for a place with the Downings, one of the most popular groups of that decade. Remaining with the group for seven years, she won the Dove Award for Female Vocalist in 1976.

During the 1970s and 1980s, Joy worked as a studio singer performing weekly on the Grand Ole Opry and sang with many gospel and country artists, including Dolly Parton, Porter Waggoner, Sandi Patty, Larnelle Harris, and Michael W. Smith. She continues to serve as a background vocalist on various artists' recordings and remains a part of Parton's backup group, performing most recently on the "David Letterman Show" and the "Today Show."

Joy's involvement with the Gaither Homecoming Videos and Concerts is a rebirth of sorts, reminiscent of her days of singing alongside her friends and long-time heroes. Convinced that sharing the gospel in song can bring encouragement, hope, and healing like nothing else, Joy continues to share her gift of communicating the message of a song with the Homecoming crowds, as well as sharing her writing, arranging, and directing abilities with her home church.

Together with husband, Landy Gardner, Joy leads the internationally recognized Christ Church Choir in Nashville. She has two daughters, Dionne and Lauren. Her favorite hobby these days is playing grandmother to Dionne's son, Dyson Scott.

—Laurie Winton

Larry Gatlin

May 2, 1948—

For God so loved the world, that he gave his only begotten Son, that whosoever believeth in him should not perish, but have everlasting life. John 3:16

arry Wayne Gatlin was born in Seminole, Texas. At age seven he began performing gospel songs with his younger brothers for a radio station in Abilene, Texas. As lead singer and songwriter for the Gatlin Brothers, Larry has enjoyed a phenomenal country music career spanning more than twenty-five years, but his heart has always been in gospel music. With number-one country music hits written by Larry and multiple Grammy Awards, the Gatlins are a household name in country music.

When Bill Gaither gathered the first little band of Homecoming Friends in a Nashville recording studio a few years ago, Larry Gatlin was there stirring up the excitement, singing with his gospel heroes. Later, *The Gatlin Brothers Come Home*, produced by Bill Gaither, became a best-seller in the Gaither Hall of Honor Series.

In the 1990s Larry starred in the Broadway hit, *The Will Rogers Follies*. He followed that by headlining a major theatrical production, *Civil War*. His life story, *All the Gold in California*, named for one of Larry's hit songs, was released by Thomas Nelson Publishers in 1998.

When this famous country star shows up at a Gaither videotaping with his Homecoming Friends, everyone in the studio listens in quiet awe at the vocal beauty and depth of expression coming from Larry Gatlin. These moments make me glad that years ago in Texas, we made the Gatlins' first recordings on Sword & Shield Records, owned by the Wills Family. Larry was inducted into the Texas Gospel Music Hall of Fame in 1997.

Currently Larry and the Gatlin Brothers are performing selected "Reunion Concerts" in Branson, Missouri.   *—Lou Wills Hildreth*

Karen Peck Gooch

March 12, 1960—

For I am persuaded, that neither death, nor life, nor angels, nor principalities, nor powers, nor things present, nor things to come, Nor height, nor depth, nor any other creature, shall be able to separate us from the love of God, which is in Christ Jesus our Lord. Romans 8:38–39

Born in Gainesville, Georgia, Karen Peck Gooch has redefined the word "soprano" in the southern gospel music industry. Karen attended Brenau College as an education major with a minor in music. She began her career in 1980 with Alphus Le Fevre's group and continued with the Nelons for ten years before starting Karen Peck & New River in 1991. Karen has two sisters, Sandra Peck and Susan Peck Jackson. Susan performs with Karen in New River.

New River is known for such hits as "Four Days Late," which was awarded Song of the Year twice in 2001. Many of the group's songs were written or co-written by Karen. She has been honored as Female Vocalist of the Year in 2004 with the Harmony Award; Favorite Soprano by the *Singing News* Fan Awards (eleven consecutive years); and as SGMA's Female Vocalist of the Year in 1982, 1983, 1998, and 2002.

Karen's musical influences include her mother, Sue, and her piano teacher, Eliza Feldman. Karen enjoys vocalists ranging from Janet Paschal and Céline Dion to Alison Krauss and Sandi Patty.

Her favorite song is "Amazing Grace," and she has experienced that grace in her own life. Karen explains, "I was saved at eight years old, and as a small child, God placed in my heart the desire to sing gospel music. I am very thankful to the Lord for giving me the desires of my heart. I am very blessed to travel with my husband, Rickey, and my children, along with my sister, Susan, and her family. I am living my dream."

Karen and Rickey have two children, Matthew and Kari. Rickey is the sound technician and manager for Karen Peck and New River. The Gooch family resides in Dahlonega, Georgia.   *—Celeste Winstead*

Howard Goodman

November 7, 1921—November 30, 2002

Though I speak with the tongues of men and of angels, and have not charity, I am become as sounding brass, or a tinkling cymbal. And though I have the gift of prophecy, and understand all mysteries, and all knowledge; and though I have all faith, so that I could remove mountains, and have not charity, I am nothing. 1 Corinthians 13:1–2

Bill Gaither has referred to Howard and Vestal Goodman as "National Treasures." They celebrated fifty-three years of marriage that began after singing in Nashville at the Ryman Auditorium. After that concert they drove to Tupelo, Mississippi, where they were married. The original Happy Goodman Family, founded by Howard, also lovingly known as "Happy," began singing in the 1940s. Howard taught his seven brothers and sisters—Gusssy Mae, Stella, Eloise, Ruth, Sam, Rusty, and Bobby—to sing and play instruments.

Rusty often remarked, "When Howard married Vestal Freeman, it was the smartest thing he ever did." With Rusty and Sam, they became a quartet that was awarded the first Grammy for a gospel group. The list of awards was long, but what really mattered to Howard was his family: wife Vestal, son Rick (Dianne), and daughter Vickie (Clark), four grandchildren, three great-granddaughters, and a large extended family.

Howard pastored a church in Madisonville, Kentucky, and he insisted that the Goodmans make it home in time for church after their concerts. Howard played the piano and wrote hits including "Give Up" and "I Don't Regret a Mile."

At videotapings, Bill Gaither would ask Howard to entertain, as only he could, by playing "Telling My Blues Good-bye." He laughed and said, "People enjoyed watching him play the piano more than listening." Most of us agree that watching and listening to Howard was a pleasure.

Thirteen months before Vestal joined the love of her life in heaven, she said, "When onstage with the Homecoming Friends, I reached over to hold the hand next to me, and it wasn't Howard's. I felt like the loneliest person in the world." Since Howard's last wish for Vestal was, "Sing, Baby, sing," she carried on. Perhaps they sing together in heaven now.

—Judy Spencer Nelon

Rusty Goodman

September 2, 1932—November 11, 1990

Therefore I say unto you, Take no thought for your life, what ye shall eat, or what ye shall drink; nor yet for your body, what ye shall put on. Is not the life more than meat, and the body than raiment? Matthew 6:25

C harles F. "Rusty" Goodman was born into a family of eight children in Cullman, Alabama. Rusty had a great ear for harmonies and was a driving force in creating the "Goodman sound." Most of the music recorded by the Goodmans was written by Rusty.

Rusty was nominated for and received numerous awards in his lifetime, including Dove and Grammy Awards. He was inducted into the GMA Gospel Music Hall of Fame, both as an artist and as a member of the Happy Goodman Family.

In 1958 Rusty married Billie Dumas. Their daughters are Tanya and April, and they have two granddaughters, Mallory and Aly Sykes.

Daughter Tanya remembers, "When we lived in Kentucky, the Goodman Family had a recording studio. My dad would often surprise my mom by bringing extra people home for dinner, and I don't mean one or two. It wasn't unusual for him to bring home six, eight, or ten people. Mom was always gracious and whipped up something wonderful to eat, and we'd sit around and laugh and listen to them tell their "road stories." Occasionally, Dad would get out the ice cream freezer and make a batch of his homemade ice cream. He loved to have a house full of company, especially around the dinner table."

Tanya recalls a story Rusty told about listening to the Grand Ole Opry. "He liked to put his radio, tuned to WSM, in the window then go outside and lie on the ground between his house and the neighbor's who also had a radio tuned to WSM, and listen, surrounded by sound. He was a pioneer of stereo and didn't even know it."

Rusty's favorite songs were "The Love of God" and "In the Garden." His favorite singer was Frank Sinatra.

Sam Goodman

March 19, 1931—August 5, 1991

God is our refuge and strength, a very present help in trouble.
Psalm 46:1

Born in Bremen, Alabama, Sam was one of the eight children of Drew Sam and Gussie Mae Goodman. Sam's eldest brother, Howard, began traveling as an evangelist at a young age and eventually recruited all of the Goodman siblings to sing. Various brothers and sisters made up the Happy Goodman Family. Over the years some would leave to get married or to join the military.

In 1957 after serving in the air force, Sam met Barbara Gibson at a tent meeting in Earlington, Kentucky, where the Goodmans were singing. They were married in 1957 and had sons, Drew Todd and Sam Kristin. In the early 1960s Howard, Vestal, Sam, and Rusty moved to Madisonville, Kentucky, and founded Life Temple Church. They continued singing in concerts throughout the week, rushing home for church on Sunday morning.

Sam became the comic and spokesperson for the family. He often introduced the members of the group and the songs on albums and included such recitations as "The Goodman Family Story," "Beauty of the Child," and "The Pledge of Allegiance." He also told humorous stories onstage. Sam sang with the Goodman Family into the 1980s.

In 1982 Sam received ministerial credentials. In 1990 he reunited with Howard, Vestal, and Rusty to record what would be their final album, *The Reunion*, which received a Grammy nomination that year. Sam continued to travel, preaching and singing, until his death in 1991.

Through the decades, the Happy Goodman Family received many Grammy nominations, two Grammy Awards, and sang at the White House for President Carter. In 1998 the Happy Goodman Family was honored to be inducted into the GMA Gospel Music Hall of Fame.

—Kris Goodman

Vestal Goodman

December 13, 1929—December 27, 2003

*And we know that all things work together for good to them that love
God, to them who are the called according to his purpose.* Romans 8:28

T
he name Vestal Goodman conjures up so many images—images
of a waving white handkerchief, big hair, an even bigger smile,
mischievous eyes, contagious enthusiasm for life and family
and friends, a strong voice, and an even stronger faith. If
Vestal Goodman were in your corner, you had God and Jesus and all the
angels on your side, and maybe even a coconut cake in your refrigerator.

I remember an artist get-together during GMA week sometime in
the mid-1980s. All of us were sort of wandering around the circle of
folding chairs, trying to fit in, or stand out, or whatever you do when
you want to feel like you belong to your group of co-workers (especially
when the communication lines are a little rusty or unfamiliar). Vestal
walked through the door and into that circle like the queen of the
Macy's Day Parade and lost no time gathering all of us under her wing.
She laughed and listened, shared road stories, and somehow during our
time together made all of us feel more important to God's work and
more valuable to His kingdom than any of us had felt when we walked
into that room.

In this day when youth is idolized and the aged are undervalued to
the point of becoming invisible, Vestal continually carved a broader
path and made a deeper impression on us all.

When I think of her, I'm reminded of those words of Frederick Buech-
ner: "When you remember me, it means that you carried something of
who I am with you . . . It means that even after I die, you can still see
my face and hear my voice and speak to me in your heart." Vestal, we
remember you. Your voice, your smile, your faith. Your family, your handkerchief, your love . . . until we meet again.

—Amy Grant

Buddy Greene

October 30, 1953—

As ye have therefore received Christ Jesus the Lord, so walk ye in him:
Rooted and built up in him, and stablished in the faith, as ye have
been taught, abounding therein with thanksgiving. Colossians 2:6–7

orn Lee Rufus Greene in Macon, Georgia, Buddy Greene spent his growing-up years learning songs on the ukulele and later moving on to the acoustic guitar. He immersed himself in such popular music styles of the time as Elvis, the Beatles, and Motown. Buddy developed a keen interest in the history of country, bluegrass, and rhythm and blues that is reflected in his music today.

Not only is Buddy a virtuoso on the harmonica, but he is also an exceptional guitarist, songwriter, and singer. His 1990 album, *Sojourner's Song,* brought his music to a wider, national audience when it won the 1991 Dove Award for Best Country Album. In 1992 with Mark Lowry, Buddy co-wrote "Mary, Did You Know?" The song earned him another Dove nomination and has become a Christmas standard. Kenny Rogers, Kathleen Battle, Natalie Cole, Reba McEntire, Gary Chapman, and others have recorded it.

In a recent project, *Rufus,* Buddy revisits his formative years as he combines bluegrass, blues, and the Beatles into a celebration of acoustic music. Buddy says, "It's just me having fun with some really talented friends, playing a bunch of old and new songs I like to play and remembering why I ever wanted to be a musician in the first place."

As a gospel musician, Buddy performs in a wide variety of concert events. He occasionally joins friends, Bill and Gloria Gaither, and the Homecoming crowd, as well as his good friend, author, and radio personality, Steve Brown, for seminars and special events.

Buddy and his wife, Vicki, live in Brentwood, Tennessee. They have two daughters, Erin and Georganna.

Rodney Griffin

December 16, 1966—

One thing have I desired of the LORD, that will I seek after; that I may dwell in the house of the LORD all the days of my life, to behold the beauty of the LORD, and to enquire in his temple. Psalm 27:4

There is no denying that a Rodney Griffin song has in some way touched nearly everyone who enjoys southern gospel music. From "My Name Is Lazarus" to "Faces," his lyrics and music combine to create moments that take you back to a loved one, a memory, a God who is real, and much more. At an early age Rodney's parents took him to such concerts as the Downings, the Happy Goodmans, and the Cathedrals, where he developed his love for gospel music and built the foundation for not only his songwriting but also his vocal ability.

Rodney Paul Griffin was born in Newport News, Virginia. He was saved at age twelve. "The preacher gave the invitation that night. I knew I was lost. I came forward, took his hand, and we prayed. It was a special night for our family—the preacher was my dad, Jeff Griffin."

Before Rodney ever picked up a pen to write a gospel song, he sang in high school with three other guys, called Fellowship Qt, from the Fellowship of Christian Athletes. "After college I moved back to where I was born and worked at Newport News Shipbuilding. I started writing songs at my desk. However, I wanted to sing. I joined a local group called the Galileans. I wanted to sing more. I went full-time in 1991 and joined the Brashears out of Russellville, Arkansas. That fall, I met the Dixie Melody Boys at the National Quartet Convention in Nashville and joined them soon after. After two years, I joined Greater Vision."

Rodney admits, "I guess my favorite song I've written is either 'I've Been There' or 'The Spirit of Brokenness.' Both continue to speak to me when I hear them."

He and his wife, Regina, have two daughters, Reagan and Riley.

—*Crystal Burchette*

Ernie Haase

December 12, 1964—

Humble yourselves therefore under the mighty hand of God, that he may exalt you in due time: Casting all your care upon him; for he careth for you. 1 Peter 5:6–7

orn in Evansville, Indiana, Raymond Ernest "Ernie" Haase III began his professional singing career in 1986 at the age of twenty-one when he joined the gospel group, Redeemed, headed by singer and songwriter, Squire Parsons. Redeemed toured extensively throughout the United States and Canada, and it was then that Ernie realized his calling as a full-time traveling evangelist, singing and proclaiming the Good News.

In 1990 Ernie joined the Cathedrals, his dream quartet and southern gospel's most elite and prestigious group. Ernie didn't marry the boss's daughter to get the job. He had joined the group before he met Lisa, bass singer George Younce's daughter. Ernie says "lightning flashed and thunder rolled." Eight months later they were married. Ernie and Lisa now make their home in Stow, Ohio.

Singing tenor with the Cathedrals placed Ernie on thousands of stages around the country and gave him a special place in the hearts of gospel music followers. He is a role model for the young and a torchbearer of traditional gospel music to the aged.

When the Cathedrals retired in 1999, Ernie did full-time solo work, but it wasn't long before he became a part of Old Friends Quartet. Today, Ernie sings with the group, Signature Sound Quartet, which he and George Younce co-founded. "What a Savior" and "Stand by Me" are big hits and crowd favorites for the group.

Ernie has appeared on numerous television and radio programs and is a regular on the Gaither Homecoming videos. He has received the Favorite Tenor and Horizon Awards from *Singing News*. With the Cathedrals and Old Friends Quartets, he has been nominated for several Dove Awards.

Marshall Hall

December 30, 1970—

Be careful for nothing; but in every thing by prayer and supplication with thanksgiving let your requests be made known unto God. And the peace of God, which passeth all understanding, shall keep your hearts and minds through Christ Jesus. Philippians 4:6–7

Born in Lexington, Kentucky, Marshall Kip Hall grew up singing along with his favorite Kenny Loggins and Kool & the Gang records, but it wasn't until high school that he began to view music as more than a hobby. At sixteen he attended the Kentucky Governor's School for the Arts and was inspired to follow music as his career path.

Marshall got his chance while attending college at his father's alma mater, Anderson University. During his internship at a local church, a producer approached him to sing for the famed Gaither Studios. Marshall was hooked. He soon began singing for such national clients as McDonald's, Disney, and Warner Brothers, and for such artists as Sandi Patty, Carman, and Clay Crosse.

Marshall looked to friend Benjamin Gaither to find a new creative outlet that would employ both his music and his heart for ministry—songwriting. His songs have appeared on records for Salvador, David Phelps, Point of Grace, and several Gaither Homecoming videos, including *God Bless America,* where he and Benjamin performed "Carry Us On," a tribute to the victims of 9/11.

In late 2001 Marshall's ministry took yet another turn when Mountain Park Community Church in Phoenix, Arizona, invited him to be a guest worship leader. There he found a new passion and continued leading members in worship for the next two and a half years.

In April 2003 Marshall married Lori in the nearby town of Sedona. Then in early 2004 he embarked on another adventure as baritone for the Gaither Vocal Band and has been on the road every weekend since.

Stuart Hamblen

October 20, 1908—March 8, 1989

But they that wait upon the LORD *shall renew their strength; they shall mount up with wings as eagles; they shall run, and not be weary; and they shall walk, and not faint.* Isaiah 40:31

uring the 1949 Billy Graham Los Angeles Tent Revival, Stuart Hamblen invited Graham to plug the meeting on his popular radio show. This advertisement made *Los Angeles Examiner* headlines. The meeting was held over and resulted in thousands, including Stuart, coming to know Christ. This beginning marked a long and endearing friendship between the Grahams and Hamblens.

Stuart's talent as singer, composer, and radio-movie personality began in Texas in the 1920s. After success in New York with four recordings, Stuart set out for Hollywood, where he made several movies. He was a member of the original Beverly Hillbillies cast.

During that time, he wrote and recorded such standards as "Texas Plains," "My Mary," "Golden River," and "Ridin' Old Paint." After he became a Christian, he wrote "It Is No Secret," the first song to cross the barrier from sacred to popular charts. "This Ole House," "Until Then," "Teach Me Lord to Wait," and "Open Up Your Heart" are just some of the 225 songs he composed.

Bill and Gloria Gaither often quote the words to his songs and say that they consider Stuart Hamblen to be one of the great lyricists. Stuart was inducted into the Nashville Songwriter's Hall of Fame and the GMA Gospel Music Hall of Fame. He received the Pioneer Award and has a star on the Hollywood Walk of Fame. He was married for fifty-five years to the lovely lady he referred to as "my Suzy" and had two daughters, Veeva and Lisa, seven grandchildren, and fifteen great-grandchildren.

—*Judy Spencer Nelon*

Suzy Hamblen

May 9, 1907—

For I know the thoughts that I think toward you, saith the LORD, thoughts of peace, and not of evil, to give you an expected end. Jeremiah 29:11

The Stuart and Suzy Hamblen story would make a great Christian western novel. At ninety-eight, Suzy, born Veeva Ellen Daniels in Oklahoma, is just as beautiful and charming as she was when Stuart introduced her on his radio show as "Little Miss Suzy Ashenfella." In 1933 Stuart asked his bride to spend their honeymoon rounding up wild horses in Arizona. She was up to it, all five feet of her next to this six-foot, two-inch Texan. She would spend an exciting fifty-five years at his side, proving it a match made in heaven. They hosted radio shows, wrote hit songs, entertained, and raised prize horses—just a typical day in the lives of these two colorful characters.

Stuart didn't care much for the business side of their endeavors. He loaded the horses and coon dogs to take them into the wild. His little Suzy usually went with him, but sometimes she stayed home to take care of the family and business. It paid off. While out riding on horseback one day, Stuart happened upon the spot that inspired him to write one of his biggest George Younce (the Cathedrals) hits: "This Ole House."

By creating a cozy home life, Suzy should be given credit for another of Stuart's compositions. As he heard their grandfather clock striking twelve at midnight, the words came: "The chimes of time ring out the news another day is through," the opening line to "It Is No Secret." For twenty-five years they lived in the Hollywood Hills home they bought from the legendary Errol Flynn and were famous for their parties.

They have two daughters, Veeva Suzanne and Lisa Obee, seven grandchildren, and fifteen great-grandchildren. Today Suzy is known by the beloved title of Nana. She still raises prize-winning Peruvian Paso horses in Santa Clarita, California.

—*Judy Spencer Nelon*

Larnelle Harris

July 11, 1947—

Being confident of this very thing, that he which hath begun a good work in you will perform it until the day of Jesus Christ.
Philippians 1:6

 arnelle Harris was born in Danville, Kentucky. He graduated from Western Kentucky University and in 1999 received an honorary doctor of music degree from Campbellsville University.

Over the years, Larnelle has consistently maintained a sound and identity distinctly his, while remaining a vital and hugely popular part of the world of popular music. He has recorded over eighteen albums and received five Grammy and eleven Dove Awards.

Larnelle says, "Every time I read a Scripture that I've heard countless times before, I always get something new out of it. Where I am with the Lord and where I am musically have a strong correlation. If I'm standing still in my walk with Him, I'm probably standing still creatively. So I'm going to continue the same trek I've tried to stay on all along, panting after the Scripture and the things of the Lord, constantly challenging myself to grow in Him—not music. With that as the focus and priority, growth and newness will inevitably be reflected in my music. That's always been the case, because He is the ultimate Creator."

Larnelle doesn't consider the story of his life to be very interesting, but the story of what the Lord has done in his life and in his heart is the story he has to tell.

Larnelle is a deacon in the church in Louisville, Kentucky, that he and his family have attended for over thirty years. Married to Cynthia and father of Lonnie and Teresa, Larnelle is an avid golfer and an expert ham radio operator. He has composed over thirty songs.

Joel Hemphill

August 1, 1939—

But without faith it is impossible to please him: for he that cometh to God must believe that he is, and that he is a rewarder of them that diligently seek him. Hebrews 11:6

J oel Wesley Hemphill was born in Fresno, California. His father, W. T. Hemphill, loved to sing. He sang when he was happy, and he sang when he was sad. Joel remembers the music of the church being an important part of his life. At the age of five Joel's family moved to West Monroe, Louisiana, where his father founded and pastored a local church. When Joel was in his teens, he played the electric guitar and later served under his father as an associate pastor.

Immediately after high school graduation and one month before his eighteenth birthday, Joel married LaBreeska Rogers after a brief courtship. They soon launched into an evangelistic ministry. Just before their third child was born, Joel began pastoring a small church in Bastrop. After ten years of fairly typical family and church life, Joel became restless and sought further direction from the Lord. It was at this time that Joel began to write gospel songs. Over the years many groups have recorded the songs that God inspired Joel to write. Among those groups are the Blackwood Brothers, the Speer Family, the Gaithers, the Florida Boys, and the Cathedrals.

For twenty-one years Joel and LaBreeska traveled with their three children, Joey, Trent, and Candy. Now they are back to their beginnings, just the two of them, carrying on the ministry they love and to which they were called: singing and preaching the gospel.

LaBreeska Hemphill

February 4, 1940—

Delight thyself also in the LORD; and he shall give thee the desires of thine heart. Psalm 37:4

L aBreeska Rogers was nine years old when she made her gospel music debut on the stage of the famous Ryman Auditorium in Nashville, Tennessee. LaBreeska was born in the small mining town of Flat Creek, Alabama. As a member of the Happy Goodman Family, her mother Gussie Mae was a sister of Howard, Rusty, and Sam. Early in her life LaBreeska, learned about the music of the church. Her father, Walter Erskine Rogers, played the guitar in their church and occasionally accompanied the Goodman Family when they sang on specials. Raised by two grandmothers who loved the Lord and family, LaBreeska grew up in an atmosphere of Christian faith, values, and music.

In 1957 LaBreeska met and married Joel Hemphill. When their first child, Joey, was only six weeks old, they began a ministry of singing and preaching. They signed their first recording contract in 1966. The Hemphills are the parents of Joey, Trent, and Candy, who until 1990 traveled and sang with their parents, making them one of the foremost mixed groups in gospel music. Now LaBreeska and Joel continue their ministry as they began: just the two of them.

Joel wrote many of the songs they sing. The group has received six Dove Awards for their efforts, and Joel has been nominated ten times by the GMA as Songwriter of the Year. Familiar titles include "Every Need Supplied," "Master of the Wind," "Consider the Lilies," and "I Claim the Blood."

LaBreeska and Joel have recorded over twenty-seven albums and have had numerous number-one and Top-Ten hits.

Jake Hess

December 24, 1927—January 4, 2004

I can do all things through Christ which strengtheneth me.
Philippians 4:13

 ake's vocal style and influence came from his father, who told him singing was talking on key and the most important thing in a gospel song was the words—and singing them clearly.

Born in Mt. Pisgah, Alabama, Jake was the youngest of twelve children. He started singing at age five with the Hess Brothers Quartet, and at sixteen, left home to join the John Daniel Quartet. He met his lifelong friend, J. D. Sumner, while singing with the Sunny South Quartet. In 1948 as lead singer, he joined pianist Hovie Lister to organize the Statesmen Quartet. Jake often said, "If there weren't a Hovie Lister, nobody would ever have heard of Jake Hess." In 1963 Jake founded the Imperials, one of the first-ever contemporary groups that began a new gospel era still celebrated today.

Jake was Elvis Presley's all-time favorite singer. Jake and the Imperials sang on Elvis's Grammy-winning gospel album, *How Great Thou Art.* Elvis even tried to sing like Jake, who would later sing at Elvis's funeral.

In 1952 Jake creatively popped the question to Joyce McWaters, the love of his life, when he asked, "Would you like to be buried with my people?" She waited until their second date to say, "Yes." Their three children, Becky, Chris, and Jake, Jr. gave them ten grandchildren and one great-grandchild.

At Jake's memorial service, Bill Gaither was emotional when he spoke of his "best friend" and shared how he admired the way Jake gave credit to someone other than himself whenever he was given a compliment. Bill finished his tribute by saying goodbye to one of gospel music's finest gentlemen, "The good news is this . . . he is singing better than he's ever sung before . . . and I think he's smiling even more broadly, too."

—Judy Spencer Nelon

Judy Martin Hess

May 3, 1971—

I will give thee thanks in the great congregation: I will praise thee among much people. Psalm 35:18

J udy Lynn Martin was born in Hayward, California, and at the age of six moved to Hamburg, Arkansas, where she grew up the younger sibling of Jonathan and Joyce. Judy was first influenced by local and regional musical groups and later by some of the well-known names in southern gospel music.

Those artists made an impression on Judy that influenced the talents already being developed at home with her parents' involvement and encouragement. Practicing at home, without a piano of their own, the Martins perfected their signature blend, a blend that would one day place them on the Gaither Homecoming stage, in the White House, on the platform of Carnegie Hall, and on television around the world.

Judy's soothing voice, tight blends, joyful countenance, and genuine smile were integral to the Martins' successes that include eight Dove Awards, a Grammy nomination, and numerous top-selling records, in addition to their many hits. Along with the Martins, Judy has set precedents in the southern gospel community, taking traditional harmony and life-altering messages to new audiences, large venues, and many young listeners.

"Choosing a favorite song is like trying to choose a favorite scripture," Judy says. "There are so many songs that have convicted me, blessed me, comforted me, and given me hope . . . songs are such a major part of my life . . . when words are not enough, a song can often reach those unreachable places in our hearts and even in our minds."

Judy is married to W. Jake Hess, Jr., son of the legendary and honored singer, Jake Hess. They have three children—Jake Hess III ("Trip"), Hannah Joyce Hess, and Emily Estelle Hess.

—Celeste Winstead

Lou Wills Hildreth

July 13, 1928—

For God hath not given us the spirit of fear; but of power, and of love, and of a sound mind. 2 Timothy 1:7

Born in Memphis, Texas, Lou was a member of the Texas First Family of Gospel Music, the Wills Family. Lou has been a television host, songwriter, publisher, journalist, industry leader, and has served for twenty years on the GMA board. She is a passionate supporter of the SGMA Hall of Fame at Dollywood. In 1998 Lou was inducted into the Texas Music Hall of Fame, and in 2004 she was the recipient of the first James Blackwood Award.

Lou received an honorary doctorate of sacred music from Louisiana Baptist University, and the Crabb Family recognized her dedication to the youth of gospel music by honoring her with the first Golden Crabb Award. Lou was the first woman to own a gospel music artist booking agency and was Mark Lowry's first agent. The Lou Hildreth Award—recognizing excellence within the gospel music industry—is presented during the Diamond Awards at the National Quartet Convention. In 2005 Lou was inducted into the Gospel Music Association Hall of Fame.

Always smiling, Lou is the redhead seen on many of the Gaither Homecoming videos. Having hosted "Wills Family Inspirational Time" in the 1960s, one of the original syndicated shows, she is a veteran of gospel music television. In the 1970s and 1980s, she hosted a daily television show in Nashville and was a Dove Award nominee.

Currently, Lou is host of "Hill County Gospel TV" and co-host of "Inside Gospel" with J. P. Miller. Her travels with husband Howard are chronicled in the *U.S. Gospel News*. She is the first to give credit to another and to give praise to God. Lou Wills Hildreth is a shining example of a lifetime committed to sharing the gospel through the power of a gospel song.

—*Judy Spencer Nelon*

Jim Hill

November 2, 1930—

In my Father's house are many mansions: if it were not so, I would have told you. I go to prepare a place for you. And if I go and prepare a place for you, I will come again, and receive you unto myself; that where I am, there ye may be also. John 14:2–3

James Vaughn Hill was born and reared in Portsmouth, Ohio. It was a Christian home where his family enjoyed gathering around an old upright piano and singing from a James D. Vaughn convention book. Jim's parents selected his name from that book. His father led singing and taught the Bible class at the local Baptist church. When Jim was sixteen, he and three friends were converted at a Baptist camp meeting. They formed the Camp Meeting Boys Trio. It was Jim's first experience with singing before a congregation.

After he was discharged from the Army in 1954, Jim formed the Golden Keys Quartet. Danny Gaither soon joined the group and added to their success. After they sang for the morning worship service at the National Quartet Convention, all the pros were asking where they were getting their new music. Jim told them that Danny's brother, Bill Gaither, was writing it. He laughs now as he remembers their question, "Who is Bill Gaither?"

In 1962 Jim joined the Stamps Quartet, his first professional venture. The Blackwood Brothers had just bought the Stamps Quartet Music Company in Dallas and needed a quartet to represent them. As manager, Jim worked with and helped start such young singers as Terry Blackwood, Mylon Le Fevre, Roger McDuff, and John Hall. In 1968 he was asked to join the Statesmen Quartet.

Jim believes that the most rewarding of all his accomplishments has been songwriting. "What a Day That Will Be" and "Precious Jesus," co-written with Gloria Gaither, appear in church hymnals.

He and his wife, Ruth, live in Middletown, Ohio, near daughter Susan and grandchildren, Melissa and James Michael.

Jim's favorite song is "Great Is Thy Faithfulness."

Stephen Hill

October 2, 1956—

Make a joyful noise unto the LORD, all ye lands. Serve the LORD with gladness: come before his presence with singing. Psalm 100:1–2

orn in Kirksville, Missouri, Stephen grew up in Greenville, South Carolina. Christian, family man, singer, songwriter, and guitarist all describe Stephen. As a backup singer, his credits range from Dolly Parton, Aaron Tippin, Hank Williams, Jr., Don McLean, Mark Lowry, Jake Hess, and Ben Speer to Marie Osmond and John Starnes. His versatility and background have served him well in presenting a varied musical palette for his listeners.

Stephen is best known for his appearances on Gaither Homecoming videos but now concentrates on his own ministry. Stephen has three solo projects. *Nothing in the World* contains songs written by Stephen and features his latest single, "I Wonder."

Stephen was saved and baptized at the age of seven but fell away from the Lord and church in his teen years. Not until he was an adult did Stephen realize he was missing many blessings by a very close margin. One night he found himself on his knees crying out to the Lord. That cry was heard and Stephen knew the Lord had been waiting for his return. As Stephen looks back on the time he calls his "wasted years," he sees where the Lord had His hand on him and was patient as He guided and corrected him. Stephen is glad that the Lord is long-suffering with us. Stephen says that he is just another example of a "prodigal son come home." He still has a long way to go, but he now relies on the Lord for guidance and direction. Stephen remains committed to sharing his gifts for the Lord. "If I get people to focus on Jesus through my talents, I feel I have done my job correctly."

Stephen and his wife, Kathy, have three children, Melody, Miriam, and Caleb.

Kenny Hinson

October 17, 1953—July 27, 1995

Great is the LORD, and greatly to be praised in the city of our God, in the mountain of his holiness. Beautiful for situation, the joy of the whole earth, is mount Zion, on the sides of the north, the city of the great King. Psalm 48:1–2

enneth Duane Hinson, the seventh child of Cecil and Stella Hinson, was born in Santa Cruz, California. When he was a child, Kenny suffered from anemia and severe bronchitis that left his lungs permanently damaged with scar tissue. Not until he was nearly a teenager did his health improve. Kenny was reared in a Christian home where he learned that it would take both persistence and courage to receive what he needed from God.

His minister father shared the knowledge of Scripture and faith in Christ, and his mother cultivated Kenny's God-given talent for music. She simply showed him how to place his fingers on the strings of the guitar, and that was all that was necessary. He joined the ensemble at church not long after that.

With brothers, Ronny and Larry, and sister, Yvonne, Kenny helped start the Singing Hinson Family when he was fourteen. Kenny was the guitar player. In the late 1970s Kenny finally realized that his vocal attributes were more important than his guitar-playing abilities. His style of music came to be known as country gospel.

The *Singing News* presented Kenny with the award for Favorite Male Vocalist of the Year in 1976. He was also awarded favorite tenor for three years. As co-writer, Kenny composed three number-one songs: "Call Me Gone," "I'll Never Be over the Hill," and "Oasis."

Kenny married Debbie, and they had two children, Kenneth and Amanda. Kenny passed away in 1995, but his legendary sound is still with us.

Ronny Hinson

October 29, 1946—

For the LORD hath redeemed Jacob, and ransomed him from the hand of him that was stronger than he. Jeremiah 31:11

Born in Freedom, California, Ronny was the fifth of eight children. He was reared in a Pentecostal preacher's home by parents who held tight yet gentle hands on the kids they always referred to as "gifts from God." Ronny attributes his songwriting, both desire and style, to his deeply spiritual upbringing and to the principles and standards demonstrated by his godly parents and expected of him and his siblings.

His life experiences, both highs and lows, have served to fuel his desire to write the prolific lyrics that show the way God will bring a person from the valley to the mountaintop.

Ronny founded the Original Hinsons on December 12, 1967, when he coaxed his three younger siblings to the platform in a small church in Watsonville, California. This coaxing began a journey to the top of the gospel music field, where they have influenced countless lives. They are recognized today as "trendsetters," after whom many singers and writers have fashioned their styles.

Ronny has a daughter, Kimberly, a son, Bo, and four grandchildren. Kim has a beautiful voice and on occasion has filled in for Bo's wife, Rhonda, in the New Hinsons.

Daughter-in-law Rhonda's ability to sing, and the fact that she and Bo are rearing their children in a Christian atmosphere, gives strong indications there could be a third generation of Ronny's dream—that the Hinson version of the gospel in song will echo for years to come.

Some of Ronny's best songs, including "Oasis," "Old Ship of Zion," and "Speak the Word, Lord," have become number-one hits for the New Hinsons.

Today, Ronny has a successful solo ministry.

Claude Hopper

October 8, 1937—

What shall we then say to these things? If God be for us, who can be against us? Romans 8:31

Born in Madison, North Carolina, Claude Hopper has become an entrepreneur and legend in the world of southern gospel music. An influential businessman, Claude founded the group originally known as the Hopper Brothers and Connie. Connie later became his wife, and together they are the foundation of one of the most successful and respected family groups in the industry.

Claude also serves on the board of directors for the National Quartet Convention. He has been an integral part of the Canadian Fan Festival as well as the Great Western Fan Festival. Claude has a rich history in music publishing and founded Hopper Brothers and Connie Publishing. In 1990 he received special recognition from North Carolina Senator Jesse Helms and Governor Jim Martin for three decades of contributions to the gospel music community. In 1999 Claude received an honorary doctorate of music. He is a founding member of the North Carolina Gospel Music Hall of Fame.

Claude's leadership has contributed greatly to the Hoppers' ministry and success. He has been greatly influenced by the Statesmen, the Blackwood Brothers, Homeland Harmony, the Speer Family, J. D. Sumner and the Stamps, and the Goodman Family. His favorite songs are "Jerusalem," "Here I Am," and "Shoutin' Time."

With appreciation Claude states, "I was able to travel and sing with my brothers for many years, and God has allowed me to continue to travel and sing with my immediate family."

Claude and his wife, Connie, have two sons, Dean and Mike, and two granddaughters, Karlye and Lexus.

—*Celeste Winstead*

Connie Hopper

July 16, 1940—

I am the vine, ye are the branches: He that abideth in me, and I in him, the same bringeth forth much fruit: for without me ye can do nothing. John 15:5

Connie Hopper is one of the most respected women in southern gospel music. A rock and foundation for the multiple award-winning Hoppers, Connie Elizabeth Shelton was born in Rockingham County, North Carolina. Early in her life, the Speer Family, the Goodman Family, Patti Paige, the Platters, and Rosemary Clooney influenced her.

Connie is now inspiring her fans not only through her music ministry but through her character and walk of faith. Her presence is one of fortitude and joy; whether times are good or bad, she seems to "know in whom she has believed." Her sincerity, warmth, and charm have made her a constant friend. Her tears fall quickly with tenderness when she shares subjects close to her heart.

In May of 2003 Connie, also a noted writer, graduated from Oakland City University with a degree in religion. She has penned more than fifty songs throughout her career. She authored a testimonial book, *The Peace That Passeth Understanding*, detailing the story of her bout with cancer and God's healing. She has written a daily devotional book, *Heart of the Matter*, and has spoken at numerous women's conferences.

Connie, whose favorite song is "Who Am I?" has been awarded the Queen of Gospel Music Award twice and the Favorite Alto of the Year and Favorite Female Vocalist of the Year Awards many times. She received the prestigious *Singing News* Marvin Norcross Award in 1998.

Connie married Claude Hopper, and they are the parents of Dean and Mike. They have two granddaughters, Karlye and Lexus.

—Celeste Winstead

Dean Hopper

October 24, 1962—

Rejoice in the Lord alway: and again I say, Rejoice. Let your moderation be known unto all men. The Lord is at hand. Philippians 4:4–5

laude Dean Hopper was born in Reidsville, North Carolina, and grew up in Madison, North Carolina. His love and knowledge of southern gospel music began as a child when he listened to the music of the Happy Goodmans, the Speer Family, and the Cathedrals. The son of Connie and Claude Hopper of the Hoppers Brothers and Connie, Dean joined the group as a drummer. In 1981 he became the lead vocalist, and more than twenty years later he continues to share the stage nightly with one of the most legendary southern gospel family groups, the Hoppers.

Dean has received multiple nominations for Lead Vocalist of the Year, and he won the Outstanding Young Man of America Award. Recently he and his brother, Mike, opened a full-service recording, mastering, and digital editing facility—The Farm—near their home in North Carolina.

Dean is a businessman and the driving force behind the scenes for the Hoppers. He married award-winning Kim Greene, popular soprano for the Greenes. Not long afterward, Kim joined the Hoppers to round out the family group. Dean and Kim have two daughters, Karlye and Lexus.

Dean shares, "I am very appreciative for the salvation I have in Christ. The opportunities to be used by the Lord are sometimes very obvious but sometimes quite subtle. I thank God for his forgiveness." Dean's favorite song is "The Old Rugged Cross Made the Difference."

—*Celeste Winstead*

Kim Hopper

May 25, 1967—

I am crucified with Christ: nevertheless I live; yet not I, but Christ liveth in me: and the life which I now live in the flesh I live by the faith of the Son of God, who loved me, and gave himself for me.
Galatians 2:20

im Greene was born in Boone, North Carolina, and grew up singing with her brothers, Tony and Tim. Surrounded by music at an early age, Kim knew she wanted singing as her vocation. Her vocals contributed greatly to the success of the Greenes in their early years. They became known for such hits as "It Sure Sounds Like Angels to Me" and "There's a Miracle in Me."

After singing with her family for ten years, Kim met Dean Hopper of the legendary Hoppers. Kim and Dean married, and Kim eventually became the fourth member of the Hoppers. Her soprano tones took on an entirely new dimension as she prepared to sing in a higher range than her usual, taking the Hoppers to even greater distinction with such songs as "Shoutin' Time," "Yes I Am," "Jerusalem," and many more. Kim also recorded a solo project, *Imagine*, which captured more of the depth and versatility of her vocal skills.

Kim has been awarded Favorite Female Vocalist nine times and Soprano of the Year eight times. Her favorite song is "These Are They." Musical influences include her family, the Rambos, and Dolly Parton.

Kim does not take family lightly. She describes family life: "Growing up in a singing family was and still is a very special thing. Even now at Christmas and at other family gatherings, we have to sing a little. I think maybe God was preparing me with music for the rest of my life even when I was a child, because now I sing with my husband; and I plan to hand the tradition on to my children."

Kim continues, "I believe God has given the gift of being able to paint the picture of what I am singing. I am thankful every day that we can touch the lives we sing to."

Kim and Dean are the proud parents of Karlye Jade and Lexus Jazz.

—*Celeste Winstead*

Benjamin Isaacs

July 25, 1972—

That if thou shalt confess with thy mouth the Lord Jesus, and shalt believe in thine heart that God hath raised him from the dead, thou shalt be saved. Romans 10:9

Benjamin Joseph Isaacs, affectionately called Gentle Ben, is the oldest child of Lily and Joe Isaacs. He was born in Middletown, Ohio, and reared in nearby Morrow. His father, Joe, formed the Calvary Mountain Boys and traveled to area churches. Between 1972 and 1975 Joe and Lily became the parents of Ben, Sonya, and Rebecca.

Young Ben was first influenced musically by his mom and dad. Later, he became interested in the styles of such gospel and bluegrass singers as Tim Caudill, Ricky Skaggs, Roy Husky, Jr., Bob Moore, and Vince Gill. This stand-up bass player has become one of the most in-demand musicians and has played with Tony Rice, Ralph Stanley, Aubrey Haynie, and Rhonda Vincent.

The Isaacs have been nominated for Grammy and Dove Awards and a host of others. Because they helped build a bridge between bluegrass and southern gospel music by combining stunning, folk-influenced harmonies with excellent instrumentation and award-winning songs, their story is one of the most compelling in any music field.

Ben composed "The Least I Can Do," "A Portion of Love," and with his sister, Sonya, "From the Depths of My Heart." His favorite song is "Go Rest High on the Mountain."

Ben began appearing with the Isaacs on many of the Gaither Homecoming videos. Also, the Isaacs have appeared periodically in the Homecoming Concert Series and joined the tour full-time in 2003.

Ben is the father of a daughter, Cameron.

Lily Isaacs

September 20, 1947—

Behold, how good and how pleasant it is for brethren to dwell together in unity! Psalm 133:1

ily Fishman Isaacs was born in Munich, Germany, just after the end of World War II. She was the immigrant daughter of Jewish Holocaust survivors from Poland.

Lily was working at Gerde's Folk City in New York when she met Joe Isaacs. This favorite hotspot launched the careers of Bob Dylan and Peter, Paul, and Mary. Joe was playing in a group called the Greenbriar Boys. Married in 1970, their first child, Ben, was born two years later, followed in 1974 by Sonya and by Rebecca in 1975. From 1972 to 1986, Joe led a group called Joe Isaacs and the Sacred Bluegrass. During this time the children exhibited a knack for harmony, almost singing before they could talk.

By 1986 they had become a family band and were calling themselves the Isaacs. The mixture of Lily's folk music with Joe's traditional mountain, bluegrass style was a big influence in their unique sound.

Early days of traveling in a station wagon yielded to van travels, with a cooler of sandwiches for economy. Lily did the booking until they hired an outside agent in 1992. A turning point in 1993 brought a landmark year: The Isaacs became so popular on the Grand Ole Opry that they were invited back numerous times.

After the Isaacs were invited to become part of the Gaither Homecoming videos, Bill Gaither stated, "Their performances are fast becoming one of the most anticipated portions of our events."

Sonya Isaacs

July 22, 1974—

I can do all things through Christ which strengtheneth me.
Philippians 4:13

orn in Middletown, Ohio, Sonya was reared in Morrow, Ohio. She was influenced musically by Emmylou Harris, Ricky Skaggs, Céline Dion, Ralph Stanley, and New Grass Revival. Sonya is a member of her family's southern gospel group, the Isaacs. The group has earned accolades and respect from all corners of the music world. Early on, along with her brother and sister, she learned to play a number of instruments. When the group's mandolin player left, rather than hiring someone to fill the gap, Sonya started playing. According to her mother, Lily, "she worked really hard and quickly learned to play."

Sonya has enjoyed a great deal of solo success including several country singles, a tour with Vince Gill, and both live and studio work with Dolly Parton, Ralph Stanley, Reba McEntire, Brad Paisley, and others. With brother, Ben, she wrote "From the Depths of My Heart," the group's first number-one hit, which brought a huge amount of attention and popularity. Both *U.S. Gospel News* and the *Gospel Voice* Awards named it Song of the Year. With her sister, Rebecca, Sonya has also written "Stand Still," as well as "Friend to the End" and "He Understood My Tears." Her favorite song is "The Love of God." In 1994 Sonya was named Horizon Award winner by *Singing News.*

The Isaacs continue their highly popular performances at bluegrass festivals, concert halls, fairs, and churches, currently in one of the busiest times of their career. Sonya says, "We are able to cross the lines of style because my family is all acoustic and even bluegrass, yet we do a lot of gospel music. It's pretty neat to be recognized in so many genres of music all at the same time."

Susan Peck Jackson

February 4, 1957—

Ask, and it shall be given you; seek, and ye shall find; knock, and it shall be opened unto you. Matthew 7:7

Susan and her sister, Karen, grew up listening to southern gospel music in Gainesville, Georgia. Another sister, Sandra, makes a trio of girls in the family. Susan made a commitment to the Lord at the age of seven. Karen taught Susan to sing alto, and Karen and their mom, Sue, have both been very influential in Susan's singing career. That influence has multiplied as Susan shares the gospel through music with Karen Peck & New River. Susan's favorite groups were the Kingsmen Quartet, the Happy Goodman Family, and the Hinsons.

New River is known for hits that include "When Jesus Passes By," "God Still Answers Prayer," "Four Days Late," "I Wanna Know How It Feels," "God Likes to Work," and many more. New River has had numerous nominations and Song of the Year Awards. Susan was honored for two years consecutively as the SGMA Female Singer of the Year.

In September 1995 Susan married David Jackson, the son of the legendary Shot Jackson, who was a member of WSM's Grand Ole Opry and a Country Music Hall of Fame inductee. Owner and builder of the famous "Sho-Bud" guitars, David is supportive of Susan's ministry through music. They have one son, Joseph.

Susan has appeared in several Gaither Homecoming videos. She is grateful to the Lord for the life she enjoys, stating, "I spent most of my adult years building a career in business and even owned a dump truck hauling business. However, in January 1991, the Lord opened the door for my sister, Karen, and me to start a new ministry, Karen Peck & New River. Since that time, I've sold my business, gotten married, and now have a son. I thank God for allowing me to sing and travel with my family."

—Celeste Winstead

Bob Johnson

November 10, 1931—

The LORD thy God in the midst of thee is mighty; he will save, he will rejoice over thee with joy; he will rest in his love, he will joy over thee with singing. Zephaniah 3:17

 orn in Greensboro, North Carolina, Bobby Gray Johnson accepted Christ at the age of fourteen. He began singing in high school and later sang with a gospel quartet in his hometown. Penny and Floyd Andrews, the Gethsemane Quartet, and the Speer Family influenced Bob musically.

Bob joined the marines in January of 1951 and spent eleven months in Korea. He received the Korean Service Medal with three stars, the Good Conduct Medal, the Presidential Unit Citation, the United Nations Service Medal, and a Purple Heart. He was discharged in January of 1954.

Bob met Jeanne in August of 1959 at a concert in Greensboro. When he saw her, he said, "Anyone that pretty who sings that well should be married to me." They were married about four months later on December 20, 1959.

Bob and Jeanne joined the Speer Family in September of 1967, and Bob drove the bus and sang with the group. He left the group in 1972 to manage jewelry stores.

In 1978 Bob began working for the PTL Television Network, and about eleven years later, Bob and Jeanne started their full-time ministry. In 1991 they formed the Johnson Family Ministries, Inc., where they are still serving, mostly in churches. Bob was ordained into the ministry that same year.

Bob and Jeanne have a daughter, Sonja Reni, who is married to Heath Nestor. Sonja and Heath have two daughters, Kylie and Kaylie.

Bob's favorite song is "The Old Rugged Cross."

Jeanne Johnson

June 16, 1941—

And we know that all things work together for good to them that love God, to them who are the called according to his purpose. Romans 8.28

eanne Poteat was born in Greensboro, North Carolina. After her parents divorced when she was five years old, she went to live with her grandparents. One day she and her brother were dropped off at their grandparents' home, and their parents never came back for them. Jeanne's grandparents took her to church for every service. "That's where I learned that God really loved me."

Jeanne took piano lessons when her grandmother could save a little of her hard-earned cotton mill earnings. Her piano teacher, Ethel Reynolds, was a great influence on Jeanne's life. She "picked me up on my lunch break at school, took me home, gave me a lesson, and then took me back to school. You think God had a plan for my life?"

Floyd and Penny Andrew and the Gethsemane Quartet also mightily influenced Jeanne. She was asked to join the quartet where she met Bob Johnson a few months later.

Bob and Jeanne were married in 1959. They have a daughter, Sonja Reni, who is married to Heath Nestor. Sonja and Heath have two daughters, Kylie and Kaylie.

Bob and Jeanne joined the Speer Family in 1967 and were with them for eight years. Many of those years the group received the Dove Award for "Best Mixed Group." They were with the Speers when they introduced Bill and Gloria Gaither's song, "The King Is Coming." Jeanne says that moment is still one of the high points of their career. Jeanne received the Dove Award for Best Female Singer in 1975.

"One of the best things that has happened to us is the privilege of singing with Bill and Gloria Gaither and our Homecoming Friends. The Lord has blessed us with several recordings."

Jeanne shares, "My mother and daddy have both passed on, but the good news is they both accepted the Lord. I've never been able to understand their actions, but I have forgiven them."

Jimmy Jones

February 5, 1921—

*And if I go and prepare a place for you, I will come again, and receive
you unto myself; that where I am, there ye may be also.* John 14:3

 orn on a farm in Allen County, Kentucky, James Edward Jones
was the ninth child of James and Bertha Jones' eleven children. Jimmy grew up in a singing family that was taken, not
sent, to church every Sunday. At thirteen, as the senior member, he sang lead in the Midget Quartet. Sometimes the group's mode
of travel was a two-horse wagon.

Jimmy's professional singing career began in March 1944 at KTHS
radio station in Hot Springs, Arkansas, with Otis Echols and the Melody
Boys. In 1951 Jimmy moved to Dallas, Texas, and joined the Rangers
Quartet to sing bass. His next move was to Atlanta along with his
brother, Brownie, to form the Deep South Quartet. Their group worked
the regular concert circuit until 1956 when they moved to Washington,
D.C., to perform with Jimmy Dean on his popular television show.

Jimmy Jones joined the Le Fevres in 1957. During this time the
Gospel Singing Caravan debuted and toured throughout the United
States and Canada. At the same time, the Le Fevres produced and
hosted the nationally syndicated "Gospel Singing Caravan Show." On
this show Jimmy performed his famous recitations in a segment called
the Poetry Corner.

Jimmy retired from the road in 1968 to live in Atlanta where he
owned and operated the Le Fevres Sing Publishing Company and later
sold it to Rex Nelon. He was presented the Living Legend Award by
the Grand Old Gospel Reunion in 1995.

Jimmy says, "The Lord has blessed me with good health and good
friends and the privilege in my latter years to be a part of the Bill
Gaither Homecoming Friends. I thank God every day for the joy of
singing and the wonderful people with whom I have had the pleasure
of working and worshiping."

Lillie Knauls

April 30, 1938—

Behold the fowls of the air: for they sow not, neither do they reap, nor gather into barns; yet your heavenly Father feedeth them. Are ye not much better than they? Matthew 6:26

I n 1970 Lillie was an original member of the Edwin Hawkins Singers, who sold over a million albums of "Oh Happy Day." Inducted into the GMA Gospel Music Hall of Fame in 2001 as a member of the Edwin Hawkins Singers, Lillie was also a beloved part of the Audrey Mieir Sings. Her friend and mentor, Audrey, encouraged her to retire from the telephone company in San Jose, California, and to go into full-time music ministry.

Lillie lived for ten years in Hawaii, from where she could travel easily to the Orient. Lillie has referred to herself as a *Musicianary*. Her first recording on Manna Records in California introduced her talent to the Gaithers. She became the first artist on their new Paragon Records label, with Bob MacKenzie as producer.

A favorite on the Gaither Video Series, Lillie is known and loved for her big, encouraging smile, lovely hats, pretty face, and great voice that can sing any style.

Lillie says that when she was invited to a Homecoming taping, she thought she would wear a hat. Folks began telling her how much they liked her hats. Some sixty videos later, she says, "I'm known as the 'hat lady.'" Out of that experience came the opportunity for Lillie to do "Hats-on Breakfasts and Luncheons with Miss Lillie." She has even written a song called "Hattitude."

Bill Gaither knows he can count on Lillie when he suddenly hands her the microphone on any song, even without notice. Lillie is not only a gifted and popular soloist, she is a speaker around the world.

—Judy Spencer Nelon

Blessed Assurance

Fanny J. Crosby

Phoebe P. Knapp

1. Bless-ed as - sur-ance, Je - sus is mine! Oh, what a fore-taste of
2. Per - fect sub - mis-sion, per-fect de - light! Vi - sions of rap-ture now
3. Per - fect sub - mis-sion, all is at rest. I in my Sav - ior am

glo - ry di -vine! Heir of sal - va-tion, pur - chase of God,
burst at my sight! An - gels de - scend-ing bring from a - bove
hap - py and blest; Watch-ing and wait-ing, look - ing a - bove,

Born of His Spir - it, washed in His blood! This is my sto - ry,
Ech - oes of mer - cy, whis - pers of love.
Filled with His good-ness, lost in His love.

this is my song, Prais-ing my Sav - ior all the day long. This is my

sto - ry, this is my song, Prais-ing my Sav - ior all the day long.

THE HAPPY GOODMANS
Howard, Vestal, Sam
and Rusty Goodman

Johnny Minick

Suzy and Stuart Hamblen

THE CATHEDRALS
Glen Payne, Scott Fowler,
Roger Bennett,
George Younce and
Ernie Haase

Judy and Rex Nelon

Dottie Rambo

Buddy Greene

Jim Hill

THE FLORIDA BOYS
(*Back*) Josh Garner, Gene McDonald,
Glen Allred and Allen Cox
(*Front*) Derrell Stewart
and Les Beasley

Mike Bowling

Doris Akers

THE LE FEVRES
(*Back Row*) Mylon Le Fevre,
Pierce Le Fevre, Jimmy Jones,
Alphus Le Fevre and Rex Nelson
(*Front Row*) Eva Mae and Urias Le Fevre

THE ISAACS
John Bowman, Lily Isaacs, Sonya Isaacs, Rebecca Isaacs Bowman and Benjamin Isaacs

Hovie Lister

THE JORDANAIRES WITH ELVIS PRESLEY
Neal Matthews, Gordon Stoker, Elvis Presley, Hoyt Hawkins and Ray Walker

Tim Riley

THE EASTERS
(*Front*) Sheri & Jeff Easter (*Back*) Charlotte Penhollow Ritchie, Madison Easter, Greg Ritchie and Morgan Easter

Lillie Knauls

THE HOPPERS
Claude, Dean, Kim, Connie and Michael Hopper

Mark Lowry

Jeanne and Bob Johnson

Mosie Lister

SIGNATURE SOUND
Roy Webb, Ryan Seaton, Tim Duncan, Doug Anderson and Ernie Haase

Sandi Patty

Larry Gatlin

Reggie and Ladye Love Smith

KAREN PECK AND NEW RIVER
Karen Peck Gooch,
Devin McGlamery and
Susan Peck Jackson

Andraé Crouch
and twin sister Sandra

THE BLACKWOOD BROTHERS
Wally Varner, Cecil Blackwood, J. D. Sumner,
Bill Shaw and James Blackwood

THE CRABBS
Jason Crabb, Kelly Bowling, Adam Crabb,
Terah Penhollow and Aaron Crabb

LaBreeska and Joel Hemphill

GREATER VISION
Jason Waldroup,
Gerald Wolfe and
Rodney Griffin

THE BOOTH BROTHERS
Jim Brady, Ronnie Booth and Michael Booth

Lynda Randle

THE MARTINS
Joyce Martin, Jonathan Martin
and Judy Martin Hess

Sue Dodge

Janet Paschal

Larnelle Harris

Stephen Hill

THE STATLER BROTHERS
Phil Balsley, Don Reid, Harold Reid and Jimmy Fortune

Ben Speer

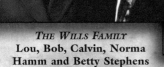

The Wills Family
**Lou, Bob, Calvin, Norma
Hamm and Betty Stephens**

The Imperials
**Armond Morales, Henry Slaughter,
Gary McSpadden,
Jake Hess and Sherrill Nielsen**

J. D. Sumner and The Stamps Quartet
**Jim Hill, Donnie Sumner, Mylon LeFevre, Tony Brown,
Jimmy Blackwood and J. D. Sumner**

Woody Wright

How Great Thou Art

Stuart K. Hine

1. O Lord, my God, When I in awe-some won-der, Con-sid-er
2. When thru the woods and for-est glades I wan-der, And hear the
3. And when I think that God, His Son not spar-ing, Sent Him to
4. When Christ shall come With shout of ac-cla-ma-tion And take me

all the worlds Thy hands have made; I see the stars, I hear the roll-ing
birds sing sweet-ly in the trees; When I look down from loft-y moun-tain
die, I scarce can take it in; That on the cross my bur-den glad-ly
home, What joy shall fill my heart! Then I shall bow In hum-ble ad-o-

thun-der, Thy pow'r through - out The u - ni - verse dis - played.
gran - deur And hear the brook and feel the gent - le breeze.
bear - ing, He bled and died To take a - way my sin.
ra - tion, And there pro - claim, "My God, how great Thou art!"

Then sings my soul, My Sav - ior God, to Thee, How great Thou art! How great Thou art!

Then sings my soul, My Sav - ior God, to Thee, How great Thou art! How great Thou art!

Alphus Le Fevre

March 2, 1912—December 9, 1988

And now abideth faith, hope, charity, these three; but the greatest of these is charity. 1 Corinthians 13:13

 lphus Le Fevre was born in Smithville, Tennessee, to Silas and Martha Le Fevre. He was the second of ten children, all of whom liked music. With older brother, Urias, playing banjo, sister, Maude, on guitar, and Alphus with his new fiddle, the Le Fevre Trio was born.

In the early 1930s Urias and Alphus attended Bible Training School, now Lee University. In 1934 Urias married Eva Mae Whittington, who joined the two brothers, reorganizing the Le Fevre Trio. They took time off during the war when Alphus was in the army and Urias was in the navy. The two brothers accidentally ran into each other in the Philippines and were able to spend about a week together.

After the war the trio resumed their music connection. In June 1950 Alphus married his sweetheart, Ellender Smith, of Atlanta. They have two children, Maria Lee and Scott Alphus, and four grandchildren.

Alphus's accomplishments were immense: As a musician, he played guitar, fiddle, banjo, piano, dobro, steel guitar, and mandolin and was famous for his accordion music at concerts. As an arranger, he wrote four-to-eight-part vocal harmony for over 500 songs. "Keep on the Firing Line" and "Must I Go Empty Handed?"are among his standards. He also encouraged his nephew, Mylon, with his song, "Without Him."

Few people could rival the smile or the kindness of Alphus. Eva Mae remembers her brother-in-law as a person who encouraged others and never spoke an unkind word about anyone. He would say, "If you can't say something nice, then don't say anything." His life and talent contributed to the golden era of the Le Fevres.   —*Judy Spencer Nelon*

Eva Mae Le Fevre

August 17, 1917—

And we know that all things work together for good to them that love God, to them who are the called according to his purpose. Romans 8:28

va Mae Whittington was born in McCall, South Carolina. Her father was a minister, and at the age of five, Eva Mae began singing at her father's street-corner services. By six, she would sit on her father's lap to play the church's organ while he pumped the pedals.

Eva Mae was eight when she met Urias and Alphus Le Fevre. They had arrived at her father's church to give a concert. Although Urias was sixteen and Eva Mae was only eight, he knew he had met his future wife. Eight years later in 1939 Eva Mae and Urias were married and with Alphus formed the Le Fevre Trio.

During World War II while Urias and Alphus were serving their country, Eva Mae sang with the Homeland Harmony Quartet. After the war, the trio was reunited and traveled throughout North America with their wonderful southern gospel sound. During this time Mylon was born, joining siblings, Pierce, Meurice, and Andrea. Later another daughter, Monteia, was born.

Notables Jim Waites and Hovie Lister also performed with the group. With popularity growing for the Le Fevres, Eva Mae was named Queen of Gospel Music in 1954. By the late 1950s the Le Fevres were living in Atlanta where Jimmy Jones and Rex Nelon joined the group. The weekly television program, the "Gospel Singing Caravan Show" ushered in the golden era for the Le Fevres.

By 1977 Eva Mae retired from traveling, saying she was going to stay home and enjoy retirement with Urias. At this time the Le Fevres became the Rex Nelon Singers. The next year Eva Mae was given the unique honor of being the first living woman to be inducted into the GMA Gospel Music Hall of Fame. In 1988 she was inducted into the Georgia Music Hall of Fame. She has also been inducted into the SGMA Hall of Fame. Bill Gaither stated that Eva Mae's actions at the first Homecoming taping sparked the beginning of the video series.

Mylon Le Fevre

October 6, 1944—

For the LORD is good; his mercy is everlasting; and his truth endureth to all generations. Psalm 100:5

ylon Le Fevre was born into a gospel singing family in Gulfport, Mississippi. In June 1962, at the age of seventeen, Mylon joined the army, making a whopping $84.00 a month as a private. When his mom, Eva Mae, and his dad, Urias, were scheduled to sing at Ellis Auditorium in Memphis, Tennessee, for the National Quartet Convention, Mylon's mother asked Mylon to come and sing his recently composed song, "Without Him." Mylon hitchhiked the 500 miles from Fort Jackson, South Carolina, in his army uniform. Unknown to the Le Fevres, Elvis Presley was planning to record a gospel album and came to the concert to choose some songs. Elvis loved "Without Him" and recorded it on his first gospel album, *How Great Thou Art.* Over the next few years, over 100 artists recorded the song.

At the age of twenty-five Mylon was fired by his family because of his long sideburns; therefore, he formed the group that became the Atlantic Rhythm Section. Eventually he got involved with drugs. In 1980 Mylon attended a concert by the 2nd Chapter of Acts where he rededicated his life. He quit rock and roll, became a janitor at his church, and started going to Bible studies. In 1981 he formed Mylon and Broken Heart, a Christian rock band that has led over 211,000 people to a decision for Christ.

Since 1980 Mylon has released twelve CDs, traveled over two million miles, been honored with a Grammy Award and two Dove Awards, and sold more than a million records. In 1993 he was called to preach the gospel.

Mylon is now a preacher and teacher, and worshiping God has become his life-style. It is Mylon's desire that all would "taste and see that the Lord is good and his mercy endures forever."

Urias Le Fevre

January 25, 1910—August 21, 1979

For God so loved the world, that he gave his only begotten Son, that whosoever believeth in him should not perish, but have everlasting life. John 3:16

Coming from a naturally talented family, Urias Le Fevre was a professional gospel singer who managed the Le Fevres from 1921 to 1964. He and his brother, Alphus, attended what is now Lee University in Cleveland, Tennessee. As part of the Bible Training School Quartet Number Two, they began their long journey as one of the most successful and innovative gospel music groups.

Eva Mae Whittington, an accomplished alto singer and piano player, joined the duo after she married Urias in 1934. Atlanta became home for the Le Fevres in 1939. The Le Fevre Trio began performing on Radio WGST and soon expanded to include family members and other professional singers and musicians. They were called the Le Fevres.

Urias created several firsts in gospel music. He was responsible for having the first public address system as part of the concert. The Le Fevres made 78-rpm recordings in the 1940s, which helped spread the popularity of the group. By 1950 television provided even more exposure. It was then that the Le Fevres began performing on WAGA-TV in Atlanta. They later created the "Gospel Singing Caravan Show," the first gospel music television show in syndication and on concert tour.

Urias can be credited with launching many young gospel music singers. At their career's high point, the Le Fevres were traveling 100,000 miles and holding 250 concerts a year.

In the late 1970s the Le Fevres retired and sold their music businesses to Rex Nelon, a longtime member of the group. Urias and Eva Mae were inducted into the GMA Gospel Music Hall of Fame and the SGMA Hall of Fame in 1997.

Hovie Lister

September 17, 1926—December 28, 2001

For God so loved the world, that he gave his only begotten Son, that whosoever believeth in him should not perish, but have everlasting life. John 3:16

Hovie Lister was born in Greenville, South Carolina. He began playing the piano at age six. By fourteen he was accompanying the Lister Brothers Quartet, a group made up of his father and uncles. Later he played for the Le Fevre Trio, Homeland Harmony, and the Rangers Quartet. By 1948 he had organized the Statesmen Quartet and became their driving force. Hovie's flair for showmanship, his style of piano playing, and his enthusiasm as master of ceremonies, usually sounded like preaching, and it certainly stirred the soul.

Determined to have the best of the best in this new quartet, Hovie included Jake Hess, "Big Chief" Wetherington, Rosie Rozelle, and Doy Ott. Among the quartet's biggest hits were "Get Away Jordan" and "O What a Savior." They recorded dozens of albums.

In 1980 Hovie was involved in the formation of the Masters V. The group included Hovie, Jake Hess, James Blackwood, J. D. Sumner, and Rosie Rozelle. Needless to say, they were an instant hit! Even though health problems forced the group off the road, the Statesmen made a comeback in 1992 with the help of Bill Gaither.

However, in 1993 Hovie was diagnosed with throat cancer. On his birthday he had surgery and by the spring of 1994 was back out on the road, healthy again.

On the Memphis Homecoming video Hovie made everyone laugh when he said, "Had I known that young Bill Gaither was going to grow up into the highly successful man we all know now, I would have been much nicer to him back then." However, many would say, "Being nice came easy for Hovie Lister."

Hovie was married to Ethel, the love of his life, was the father of Lisa and Hovie, Jr. (Chip), and grandfather of Hovie III ("Trey") and Timothy Michael.

—*Judy Spencer Nelon*

Mosie Lister

September 8, 1921—

I can do all things through Christ which strengtheneth me.
Philippians 4:13

 ew songwriters have enjoyed the success attained by Mosie Lister. Even though he is in his eighties, he writes better than ever. Engage him in conversation, and he'll be sure to tell you that he's "not retired!" Among the many hundreds songs that have emerged from his prolific pen are "'Til the Storm Passes By," "Then I Met the Master," "How Long Has It Been?" "I'm Feelin' Fine," and "His Hand in Mine."

Born and reared in Cochran, Georgia, Mosie studied English and music in college. He credits Mr. Adger M. Pace, an early teacher, with words of wisdom about writing music. He quoted, "Be sure the tune can be whistled. Use a title people can remember. Start well and end well with something meaningful in the middle."

By the late 1940s Mosie had worked with a number of groups, including a brief tenure as an original member of the Statesmen Quartet. However, as his songs found favor, Mosie retired from the road to devote all of his time to songwriting.

In 1953 he founded Mosie Lister Publishing Company, which later merged with Lillenas Publishing. Throughout his career Mosie was known for his ability to draw from a variety of musical styles always with strong Bible-inspired, Christian lyrics. As a result, such gospel and secular artists as George Beverly Shea, Jimmie Davis, Elvis Presley, and Porter Waggoner have recorded his songs. His two favorite songs are "Amazing Grace" and "Holy, Holy, Holy," mostly because of the impact of their message.

Mosie and his wife, Martha, make their home in Brandon, Florida.

—*Bob Crichton*

Mark Lowry

June 24, 1958—

But God commendeth his love toward us, in that, while we were yet sinners, Christ died for us. Romans 5:8

Mark Alan Lowry was born in Houston, Texas and grew up there. Since age eleven he has been singing, recording albums, and making videos. In the years just after graduation he traveled to every Independent Baptist church throughout the country. At one time Mark's agent had booked him in forty-three cities in forty-one days! He developed his comedy routine to fill gaps in concerts while soundtracks were being changed. His audiences laughed as he told stories of his life and testimony.

Beginning in 1988 Mark sang baritone for thirteen years with the Gaither Vocal Band. His rapport with Bill Gaither during a concert was a hit and then became a highlight when the Homecoming Tour began. Mark has been featured on all of the Homecoming videos, often in a co-starring role with Bill.

In 1984 Mark wrote a series of questions to be used between scenes of a Christmas play. Six years later Buddy Greene wrote music for Mark's lyrics and a beautiful Christmas song was born. Including Michael English, Kenny Rogers, Wynonna Judd, Natalie Cole, Donny Osmond, and of course, Mark himself, over thirty different artists have recorded "Mary, Did You Know?"

Mark has recorded six comedy and music videos. Four of them have gone gold, and two, platinum. His most recent video, *On Broadway*, remained at the top of the *Billboard* charts for weeks.

Mark's most recent project is *Mark Lowry Goes to Hollywood*, recorded during his "God's Crazy about You" tour.

Mark's father, Charles, is an attorney in Lynchburg, Virginia. His mother, Beverly, speaks and sings at various conferences. She has been featured on two of Mark's recordings.

Bill Lyles

December 7, 1920—June 30, 1954

For I know the thoughts that I think toward you, saith the LORD, thoughts of peace, and not of evil, to give you an expected end. Jeremiah 29:11

Bill was killed in a plane crash with R W Blackwood, Sr. in 1954 near Clanton, Alabama. A crowd of 5,000 attended their funeral in Memphis, Tennessee. Bill had three sons, Bill, Jr., Gary, and Curtis. Bill, Jr. remembers getting postcards from his dad when he traveled.

Bill, Jr. says, "My dad was born James William Lyles, in Burning Bush, Georgia. He was the fourth of seven children. I don't really know where or when his interest in gospel music began, but I do know that he sang with the Hamilton Quartet in Chattanooga, Tennessee, and also with the Suwannee River Boys.

"He and my mother met in church in Chattanooga where Daddy sang in the choir. They were married in June 1940, and I came along in October 1941. We were living in Stone Mountain, Georgia, when James Blackwood contacted Daddy with an offer to join the Blackwood Brothers Quartet for a salary of $70.00 a week. I still have the telegram.

"He never wrote any music nor garnered any awards that I know of. He just happened to be the best and smoothest bass singer ever. Many, many folks have told me so, and I just happen to agree. He was a good Christian man who loved his family very much.

"Whenever he returned from a long trip, my brother and I would get up to see him regardless of the time. He always had a gift for us. I remember seeing the joy in his face during those times. When he died, it was such a great loss to my mother, Ruth, and I never understood till after she died and I read notes tucked in the Bible. I'll always wonder what life would have been like had he remained alive, but God in his infinite mercy and love took care of us."

—Bill Lyles, Jr.

Jonathan Martin

May 19, 1970—

My brethren, count it all joy when ye fall into divers temptations; Knowing this, that the trying of your faith worketh patience. But let patience have her perfect work, that ye may be perfect and entire, wanting nothing. James 1:2–4

ylma and J. W. Martin reared Joyce, Jonathan, and Judy in rural Hamburg, Arkansas, in an 800-square-foot cabin without electricity or indoor plumbing. To pass the time the young siblings began singing together coached by their musical mom who had no formal training. Jonathan recalls practicing bass guitar against a hollow interior door and using a car battery to listen to the radio; seated beside the radio he listened and learned harmony by ear. He remembers having to ration listening on Fridays and Saturdays to save the battery.

Little did they know that in just a few years friends Mark Lowry and Michael English would seize Gloria Gaither at a videotaping to audition the "Martins" in the women's restroom where the acoustics were just right. By noon the next day, Bill had invited them to sing "He Leadeth Me" on the *Precious Memories* video.

In 1988 their home state of Arkansas honored the trio with the distinguished Governor's Award of Excellence. The group is one of the most recognized in gospel music with their unique sound, which is affectionately referred to as "Martin music." Favorites include "Grace," "Out of His Great Love," and an *a cappella* rendition of "The Doxology." Including an invitation to sing for President George W. Bush at the White House, their career has been more than the family could have ever imagined.

Jonathan's faith and family values have sustained him during life's challenges. His testimony is one of courage, grace, and God's faithfulness. His songs reflect the promises that God has for all of us.

Jonathan's favorite Scripture with wife, Dara, and his four children, Halea, Taylor, Michael, and Olivia, is James 1:2, "Count it all joy!"

—Judy Spencer Nelon

Joyce Martin

January 6, 1968—

Be careful for nothing; but in everything by prayer and supplication with thanksgiving let your requests be made known unto God. And the peace of God, which passeth all understanding, shall keep your hearts and minds through Christ Jesus. Philippians 4:6–7

amed for her mother, Wylma Joyce Martin was born in Bastrop, Louisiana, and grew up in nearby Hamburg, Arkansas. Music became a central part of Joyce's life at an early age as she and her two siblings, Judy and Jonathan, were taught to sing by their mother. Joyce describes how she would "teach us the old hymns around the piano at church, and she made sure we knew our parts. We couldn't afford a piano, so we had to practice everything *a cappella.* That's how our blend grew so tight."

That blend, with a unique added twist, would one day be a signature sound for one of the most innovative groups of its time—the Martins—who epitomize what southern gospel harmony is all about. Featured regularly on the Gaither Homecoming Videos and Concerts, the Martins quickly became a crowd favorite, including not only a moving testimony for older individuals but also an inspiration to many young artists of the genre's future.

Influenced musically by Patti LaBelle and Wynonna Judd, Joyce has a voice that rings out with unbridled passion and force. Her talent as an emcee has given new life to the performance aspects of southern gospel music.

Along with Judy and Jonathan, Joyce has received a Grammy nomination and eight Dove Awards, including several Southern Gospel Song of the Year honors.

Joyce especially enjoys time with her family and states, "I have two beautiful children; Trey and Mae are little miracles that remind me every day that God is faithful. He cares about the personal desires of our hearts."

—Celeste Winstead

Babbie Mason

February 1, 1955—

I will praise thee; for I am fearfully and wonderfully made: marvellous are thy works; and that my soul knoweth right well. Psalm 139:14

L ike so many female vocalists that preceded her, Babbie Yvett Robie Wade began her music education in the church. There she allowed the seeds of faith to be planted and nurtured, and there they bore fruit. As a preacher's daughter from Jackson, Michigan, Babbie says, "I don't remember a time that I didn't love the Lord. It was easy to fall in love and commit to Christ: I watched my parents."

Babbie's parents, George and Georgie Wade, served in one church for nearly forty years. Shortly after giving her life to Christ at the age of eight, Babbie began serving as church pianist and choir director and did so for sixteen years. In that church Babbie began experiencing first-hand the joys of leading others in worship.

Babbie's dedication to the Lord serves as a firm foundation in her home. The Masons enjoy working together and consider themselves perfect examples of how God can use a husband-and-wife team to complement each other's strengths and weaknesses. Babbie says, "Our differences have proven to be the strength in our relationship both at home and on the road."

Living in Georgia, Babbie and husband, Charles, make it a priority to be there for their sons, Jerry and Chaz.

Such artists and groups as Larnelle Harris, CeCe Winans, Helen Baylor, Albertina Walker, Scott Wesley Brown, Truth, and the Brooklyn Tabernacle Choir have recorded Babbie's compositions. Her works have been in countless print projects, including choral octavos, musicals, hymnals, and chorus worship books.

A teacher at heart, Babbie is compelled to share her knowledge with young musicians as adjunct professor of songwriting at local colleges. She and Charles mentor hundreds of upcoming musicians at the annual Babbie Mason Music Conference.

Gene McDonald

May 3, 1965—

For the wages of sin is death; but the gift of God is eternal life through Jesus Christ our Lord. Romans 6:23

I n Kennett, Missouri, in the bootheel region, Tommy and Doris McDonald and big sister, Janeene, welcomed Gene into the family. Gene cut his teeth on gospel music when he started singing at the age of three with the family group. At six he made his first solo album. His favorite song was "When They Ring Those Golden Bells." His parents took him to singing schools and taught him to read music, harmonize, and sing the tenor part. During the summer between his junior and senior years of high school, Gene grew six inches taller and his voice changed from tenor to bass.

Along with going to every singing school in his area, Gene also attended college at Arkansas State University in Jonesboro, where he earned a degree in music education. His ability to read shaped notes along with his great bass voice endeared him to such bass singers as Rex Nelon, who introduced him to the Carol Lee Singers on the Grand Ole Opry and later to Les Beasley.

When he attended the Ben Speer Stamps School of Music, Ben noticed Gene's talent and encouraged him by letting him live in his recording studio for a while. Bill Gaither commented, "He's the best bass singer to come along in many years." Bill invited Gene to sing at his recording sessions, which led to his becoming a favorite part of the Homecoming Series.

Today Gene McDonald is an important member of the legendary Florida Boys Quartet. Les Beasley remarks, "Over the years, I've watched Gene become one of the finest bass singers in the industry."

Gene met his wife, Teri, at the Summer River Singing in Live Oak, Florida.

—Judy Spencer Nelon

Gary McSpadden

January 26, 1943—

But seek ye first the kingdom of God, and his righteousness; and all these things shall be added unto you. Matthew 6:33

ary Michael McSpadden was born in Mangum, Oklahoma, and grew up in Lubbock, Texas. Early musical influences in Gary's life were the Statesmen Quartet, the Blackwood Brothers, the Oak Ridge Quartet, Jake Hess, and Elvis Presley. As a teenager, Gary dreamed of being involved in gospel music. He joined the Statesmen to fill in for Jake Hess and soon after became a member of the Oak Ridge Quartet. Later, Gary and Jake Hess formed the Imperials.

For the first three years that Gary was lead singer for the Bill Gaither Trio, he and his father were joint pastors of a church in Fort Worth, Texas. Over the years, Bill, Gloria, and Gary recorded some of the world's best-known and most loved gospel songs.

Gary was honored when groups with which he had sung, the Imperials and the Bill Gaither Trio, were inducted into the GMA Gospel Music Hall of Fame. After Gary left the Trio to pursue a solo career, he recorded thirteen albums and began writing songs. "Jesus Lord to Me," "Hallelujah Praise the Lamb," and "Jesus Be Jesus in Me" have become familiar choruses sung in our churches.

Gary remembers, "As a child, I watched and listened to a wonderful man of God preach and live what he believed. That man was my father. What he believed, preached, and lived was the Bible . . . the Word of God. I was given a special heritage . . . the preaching and singing of the gospel of Jesus Christ. My heritage and call is to go into all the world and preach the gospel to every one. I have tried to do exactly what Christ commanded."

Gary and his wife, Carol, have two children, Shawn and Michelle, and five grandchildren.

Audrey Mieir

May 12, 1916—November 5, 1996

For unto us a child is born, unto us a son is given: and the govern-
ment shall be upon his shoulder: and his name shall be called Won-
derful, Counsellor, The mighty God, The everlasting Father, The
Prince of Peace. Isaiah 9:6

I n 1926 ten-year-old Audrey Wagner sat on the balcony stairs of Angelus Temple in Los Angeles, California, as Aimee Semple McPherson came to the platform. Great chords of music filled the place, swelling from the magnificent organ, the Silver Band, and the choir. Fifty-two hundred people packed the auditorium. Holly-wood stars and politicians rubbed elbows with common folks. Audrey dreamed of someday being on that stage, and soon she was.

She attended LIFE Bible College, and on January 1, 1936, married the love of her life, Charles Mieir, with Aimee Semple McPherson officiat-ing. God and Aimee's style and music inspired Audrey to begin composing songs. She was always grateful to her mentor, Aimee Semple McPherson.

After her mother's untimely death, Audrey went through a dry period for a year and wrote no songs. One night, she asked God to forgive her, and early in the morning she was comforted with the words that she began to compose and sing: "I'll Never Be Lonely Again."

A choir director, composer, and arranger, Audrey trained others and introduced many new, young artists, including her beloved Lillie Knauls and Andraé Crouch, who affectionately referred to her as his "great white mama." They credit Audrey with much of their success. She introduced them to her lifelong publisher, Tim Spencer, at Manna Music, where both obtained contracts and Andraé published his first song, "The Blood Will Never Lose Its Power."

Audrey developed a passion for abandoned Korean-American children and devoted her life to the Mieir Havens in Korea. She was instrumen-tal in bringing thousands of children to America for adoption.

Audrey and Charles had a son, Michael, an adopted son, Mark, and an adopted daughter, Liane, from Korea.   *—Judy Spencer Nelon*

Johnny Minick

July 8, 1955—

And I saw a new heaven and a new earth . . . Revelation 21

Born in Little Rock, Arkansas, Johnny Minick grew up in the home of Christian parents who nurtured him in godly traditions. At three he started singing and playing the guitar and by six had developed an interest in the piano and began classical training. After winning several regional and national piano competitions, he became the pianist and arranger for the Happy Goodman Family. His classical and jazz background immediately influenced the direction of the Goodman recordings.

Striking a balance between full-time music ministry and the calling to preach was difficult. In 1977 Johnny left the Goodmans to pursue the pulpit ministry he had begun at age twelve. After some years as a successful evangelist, he pioneered a church in Little Rock. During those years Johnny wrote several songs for his family group, the Johnny Minick Family, which charted nationwide.

In 1992 Johnny and his family moved to Smyrna, Tennessee, to pioneer another church, River of Life. After the loss of Rusty and Sam, the Goodmans were looking for new direction. Frequently they would drive to Smyrna to hear their friend preach. They sang in a few of those services. After appearing on Gaither videos, the Goodman Family began singing again and continued until Howard's death in 2002. Johnny's son, Aaron, picked up Howard's microphone and kept the group together until Vestal's death in 2003.

Johnny and his wife, Sherry, continue to pastor the River of Life Church in Smyrna. He is still recording and busy with a limited concert schedule, along with revivals and special events.

Johnny's favorite songs are "The Love of God" and "The Eastern Gate."

Armond Morales

February 25, 1932—

Make a joyful noise unto the LORD, all ye lands. Psalm 100:1

orn in Huntington Park, California, Armond was reared in the Assembly of God Church in Maywood, California. He began singing in the youth choir and later joined the adult choir. Armond says "I sang my first solo when I was about fourteen years old. I started out as a tenor until my voice changed, and you know the rest."

Armond's father, Alfred, came from the Philippines and met and married his mother, Alice Riddle. They had four children, Armond, Alice, Kenneth, and Pam.

Armond has been involved in gospel music since the early 1950s; in 1963 he started singing with the Weatherford Quartet in southern California. He was an original member of the Imperials when they formed in 1964. Armond's brilliant career has included working with Elvis Presley, Jimmy Dean, Carol Channing, and Pat Boone.

The groups with which Armond has sung have received Grammy and Dove Awards. With the Imperials he was inducted into the GMA Gospel Music Hall of Fame.

The song Armond loves most is "Praise the Lord." That song has touched countless people, including Armond himself. He has traveled millions of miles doing what he most loves to do—singing and ministering the gospel of Jesus Christ.

Armond has four children. The three from his first marriage are Bryan, Lisa, and Tracey. He married Bonnie in November 1970, and they have a son, Jason, who sings with the Imperials. Jason and his wife, Erin, have a daughter, Madeline, born in July 2004. Armond beams, "She's the apple of Poppy's eye."

Today Armond sings with some former members of the Imperials in a group called the Classic Imperials.

—Bonnie Morales

Joe Moscheo

August 11, 1937—

That Christ may dwell in your hearts by faith . . . Ephesians 3:17

Joe A. Moscheo II grew up in Albany, New York, and moved to Nashville in 1964. Through the 1960s and 1970s he worked as a studio musician and record producer. Because of his relationship with Elvis Presley during that time, he became involved in many other recording projects and television events. Joe was associate producer for "He Touched Me—The Gospel Music of Elvis Presley," which was a joint project between the Elvis Presley estate and Gaither Television Productions. As a member of the Imperials, Joe worked with Elvis on stage and in the recording studio from 1968 to 1972, both as a singer and keyboard player. He has maintained a lasting relationship with the Presley family and is frequently part of the ongoing Elvis celebrations around the world.

In 1978 Frances Preston, then president and CEO of BMI, hired Joe to work with songwriters and music publishers. During his sixteen years at BMI, Joe had the pleasure of being involved in all aspects of the music industry, while also cultivating a close relationship with many organizations outside the music field.

Joe produced the Dove Awards for eight years, and as a member of the Imperials, he was inducted into the GMA Gospel Music Hall of Fame. In 2004 Joe was executive producer of the GMA Gospel Music Hall of Fame Awards that aired on the TBN cable network.

From 1994 to 1996 Joe owned an artist management company and worked with BeBe and CeCe Winans, Michael English, Wynonna and Naomi Judd, and several other contemporary Christian artists.

Joe is president of MCS America, a company that administrates music copyrights and royalty payments. Other than business, Joe enjoys tennis, golf, and painting. He has been married to Judy since February 1984 and has four children and five grandchildren.

Buddy Mullins

October 23, 1968—

Make a careful exploration of who you are and the work you have been given, and then sink yourself into that. Don't be impressed with yourself. Don't compare yourself with others. Each of you must take responsibility for doing the creative best you can with your own life. Galatians 6:4–5, *The Message*

enneth Harold Mullins, or as most people know him, "Buddy," was born in Trenton, Tennessee. He began traveling full time with his family when he was eight years old. Singing quickly became his life's pursuit. Each year he seemed to be climbing farther up the ladder of success and recognition. Then one day the ladder toppled, and he had to come to terms with the difference in singing about his faith and truly living it.

God wanted Buddy to pursue Him—not just a singing career. Through this time, God made clear to him that the most important stage he would ever perform on was not in front of audiences of thousands but on the stage in his home: for the three people within the walls. God has been gracious and given him a new platform of solo ministry.

Buddy has been influenced by Kenny Hinson, Ronnie Milsap, Russ Taff, Michael English, and Don Henley. He was a member of Mullins, Mullins & Co., who won the 1992 *Singing News* Award for Favorite New Group. He was the lead vocalist for the Gaither Vocal Band from 1993 to 1995. His band, Sunday Drive, toured with Josh McDowell Ministries and various other contemporary groups. Buddy has also written many number-one southern gospel and contemporary Christian songs.

Buddy is married to Kerri Anne, and they have two daughters, Victoria Scarlet and Jaclyn Olivia.

Buddy summarizes, "No stage will ever elevate itself above my walk with Christ and my family."

Jim Murray

March 8, 1944—

The LORD is my light and my salvation; whom shall I fear? the LORD is the strength of my life; of whom shall I be afraid? Psalm 27:1

Born in Lansing, Michigan, Jimmy Kenneth Murray has always loved good, old-fashioned southern gospel music. While he was growing up, Jim immersed himself in musical opportunities.

After studying voice for two years at Michigan State University, Jim became a member of the Melodairs Quartet and later the Ambassadors Quartet. While he was singing with the Orrell Quartet in 1966, Jake Hess heard Jim's rich tenor voice and invited him to join the newly formed Imperials. During the twenty years Jim was with the Imperials, he had the opportunity to sing backup for Elvis Presley, Pat Boone, and Carol Channing.

The Imperials produced fifty albums and received five Grammy Awards and fifteen Dove Awards during the two decades that Jim was with them. After the Imperials shifted from traditional four-part harmony that had been their trademark to a more pop style, Jim decided to leave the group.

In 1988 Bill Gaither invited Jim to join the Gaither Vocal Band. His wonderful tenor voice shone on such favorites as "Wings" and "A Few Good Men," and being featured on the Homecoming Series gave him an opportunity to sing four-part harmony again.

Jim says, "I've known Bill and Gloria for many years, and I have always respected their integrity. It was a joy to be part of the Gaither team, especially the now historic video series."

Following surgery Jim thought he would never sing again. However, thanks to his doctors and to countless prayers, the Lord has allowed him to continue ministering with his voice.

Today Jim and his wife, Lorretta, live in Hawaii where he has reunited with his friends, Armond Morales and Sherman Andrus, to form the Classic Imperials.

Judy Spencer Nelon

October 7, 1944—

In every thing give thanks: for this is the will of God in Christ Jesus concerning you. 1 Thessalonians 5:18

The Peck sisters, Judy, Sharon, and Linda, were born in Valdosta, Georgia, and began to harmonize at a young age. In their preacher dad's record store in Columbus, Georgia, their inspiration came from hearing their favorite groups, the Blackwood Brothers, the Statesmen, the Le Fevres—who later became the Rex Nelon Singers—and Doris Akers. Little did Judy know that one day, as vice-president of Manna Music, she would become friends with and would publish the music of Doris Akers ("Sweet, Sweet Spirit"), Audrey Mieir ("His Name Is Wonderful"), Andraé Crouch ("Through It All"), and Stuart K. Hine ("How Great Thou Art").

In 1992 Gloria Gaither invited Judy to Nashville, where the Gaithers were taping favorite songs and singers. No one could have imagined the impact that the Gaither Video Series was about to make, not only for audiences, but also for the Homecoming Friends who really got to know each other during the taping.

In 1999 Judy married Rex Nelon with a host of those friends present. The Gaither Vocal Band, Jake Hess, Janet Paschal, Johnny Minick, and the Geron Davis Trio sang, Gloria spoke, and Amos Dodge officiated. Lifetime friend, Howard Goodman, escorted Judy down the aisle. Only ten months later, while in England for the taping of the London Homecoming video, these friends would be there to comfort Judy as Rex left this shore for heaven.

Judy concludes, "That's what this music is all about—living and dying. It's our hope and belief in the future that makes us go on." Judy lives in Nashville, where she continues her publishing, serves as the first woman president of the Southern Gospel Music Guild, and is on the Board of Directors for both the GMA and SGMA. She will quickly tell you—what she loves most is being a mom and grandma.

—Lou Wills Hildreth

195

Rex Nelon

January 19, 1932—January 23, 2000

I am the resurrection, and the life: he that believeth in me, though he were dead, yet shall he live. John 11:25

*I*nducted into the Southern Gospel Music Hall of Fame, Rex expressed gratitude for having the chance to do the music he loved. Rex joined the legendary Le Fevres in 1957. Later, when they became the Rex Nelon Singers, his daughter, Kelly, and son, Todd, joined the group along with other new, young talent. For her first concert Janet Paschal didn't appear but telephoned Rex explaining that she had gone the wrong way on the freeway. He told her: "Janet, you're fired." Since he had a reputation for being a prankster, she understood him to be kidding. Janet was followed by Karen Peck, who was followed by Charlotte Ritchie, and many others for whom Rex helped launch careers. Rex collected songs and became an outstanding publisher with copyrights to such songs as, "What a Savior," and "If We Never Meet Again."

In 1999 Rex retired but was happy to board the Gaither Homecoming tour bus when Bill invited him to sing bass at the concerts. Rex enjoyed breakfast with Bill Gaither, Jake Hess, Bob Cain, Ben Speer, and others, where they reminisced and agreed: "These are the good ole days."

These friends were present during the wedding ceremony, and in too short a time they were there again bringing comfort when Rex passed away just hours before the taping of the London Homecoming. On that video, if you look carefully, you will notice the grief on the faces of friends who had just lost one they loved; however, you can also hear the singers' song of hope concerning the future and the One who holds the future.

Rex Nelon ran his race well, and he finished well. He had started with a song, and he ended his race still singing about the Lord he loved. We miss him, but we know that we will again hear him singing.

—*Judy Spencer Nelon*

Calvin Newton

October 28, 1929—

Finally, brethren, whatsoever things are true, whatsoever things are honest, whatsoever things are just, whatsoever things are pure, whatsoever things are lovely, whatsoever things are of good report; if there be any virtue, and if there be any praise, think on these things. Philippians 4:8

esley Calvin Newton was born in West Frankfort, Illinois, son of a Pentecostal preacher who was continuously looking for work. Although his family's frequent moves were difficult for young Calvin, he found that singing in church was as natural as talking. By the time he was six he was singing with his mom and dad on a Saturday morning radio show in Harrisburg, Illinois.

In the 1940s when employment opportunities abounded, the family moved to Chicago. Calvin worked at night unloading boxcars and as the supervisor of grown men. In high school since Calvin constantly got into fights, his parents sent him to a boarding school in Sevierville, Tennessee. His love for gospel music took root while he sang at one of the finest gospel finishing schools.

Along with Jake Hess, "Big Chief" Wetherington, and Wally Varner, Calvin joined the Melody Masters. He was still in his teens when the number-one gospel group, the Blackwood Brothers, came knocking on his door.

As a past member of the Oak Ridge Quartet, Calvin was honored when the group was inducted into the GMA Gospel Music Hall of Fame. He was presented the Living Legend Award by the Grand Old Gospel Reunion.

Married since 1963, Calvin and Joyce have two children: a son, Wes, and a daughter, Jackie Newton Harling. Calvin and Joyce also have a granddaughter, Samantha.

Calvin was comforted by Jake Hess, who visited him while he was in prison and stood by him when he felt abandoned. Later, Bill Gaither invited him to be a part of the Homecoming videos; many people have been touched by Calvin's testimony.

Now, Calvin's favorite song is "Something Beautiful."

Doug Oldham

November 30, 1930—

*And we know that all things work together for good to them that love
God, to them who are the called according to his purpose.* Romans 8:28

rom the time his father, Dale Oldham, stood him on a table
at a National Youth Convention, Doug has been singing. At
the age of eight he was paid for singing "The Holy City." He
still has the silver dollar Bill Peak gave him for that performance. Doug's inspiration to sing came from his hero, Herb Thompson.
Called "gospel's great communicator," his lifelong striving to make words
meaningful came from Dr. Robert Nicholson, who gave him one verse
to sing with the Anderson College Choir. Verse four of "My Soul Is Satisfied" set his course.

Doug has traveled the world singing and has been on Christian
television for decades. He has appeared at the White House, Carnegie
Hall, Wolftrap, the Superdome, Hines Hall, Praise Gatherings, Chris-
tian Artists Seminars, CBA and NRB, and with Benny Hinn and on
Gaither Homecoming videos. He has sung for five presidents, for the
Queen of England, and for Prince Philip.

Doug has hosted three TV shows and written two books—one with
his wife, Laura Lee. He has recorded sixty-five albums, one of which
went gold. The albums have recently been remastered and put on CDs.
Doug has received two Dove Awards and two Angel Awards. Even with
all of these accomplishments, his family is his heart's joy.

Three Gaither songs, "The Old Rugged Cross Made the Difference," "Thanks to Calvary," and "He Touched Me," echo Doug's personal testimony. Doug and Laura Lee have been married since 1951
and have three daughters, three sons-in-law, and five grandchildren.
What is Doug Oldham's legacy? All these children and grandchildren
are Christians serving the Lord.

—Laura Lee Oldham

Doy Ott

April 28, 1919—November 6, 1986

Unto thee lift I up mine eyes, O thou that dwellest in the heavens.
Psalm 123:1

oy Willis Ott fell in love with southern gospel music when he first heard the Virgil Stamps Quartet on a KRLD radio broadcast in Dallas, Texas. A career as a musician, singer, and vocal arranger was the result of this influence. Doy played for a string of groups which included the Stamps-Baxter Quartet, the Melody Boys, the Hartford Quartet, and the Rangers with Arnold Hyles, Vernon Hyles, Walter Leverett, and Denver Crumpler. He also played the piano for the Homeland Harmony Quartet. While Hovie Lister served in the Korean War, Doy was invited to play for the famous Statesmen Quartet. When Hovie returned, Doy became the group's permanent baritone singer.

Hovie always appreciated Doy's versatility as an arranger and pianist. Onstage the most lively moment for the Statesmen Quartet would come when they sang their rousing spiritual, "Get Away Jordan." Hovie would jump up from the piano, Doy would slip onto the piano bench, and "Hovie Lister and the sensational Statesmen would bring down the house"—as they say in these circles.

Doy always had a smile on his face and was a quiet-natured man with kind words. He contributed much to the success of the Statesmen during the more than twenty-five years he spent with the group.

Doy was married to Mary, and they had a son named Skipper. Doy was inducted into the Southern Gospel Music Association Hall of Fame in 2000.

Ivan Parker

December 21—

For God so loved the world, that he gave his only begotten Son, that whosoever believeth in him should not perish, but have everlasting life. John 3:16

I van Parker was born in Roanoke Rapids, North Carolina. One Sunday night the pastor, Ivan's father, asked, "Does anyone have a song to sing?" Immediately, Ivan jumped off his mother's lap, ran to the microphone, and began to sing "On the wings of a snow white dove, He sends His pure, sweet love." He kept on singing until his father said, "Okay, I think that's enough." He had sung his first solo in church at the age of two. Ivan was saved in that same church when he was nine. That decision has remained steadfast throughout his life as he follows God's calling to use his talents to share the gospel of Jesus Christ.

Ivan says that his parents have been his greatest influences. His mother, Katie, always prayed that God would use her children in ministry. Ivan sees his life as a fulfillment of his father's dreams: His father was a singer and musician who put music aside when he was called to the ministry. Singers who have influenced Ivan are Bill Gaither and Jake Hess. Jake called Ivan his "favorite crooner."

Ivan says that the song, "It Is Well with My Soul," has often ministered to him, but his all-time favorite song is "Midnight Cry." He has been part of fifty-eight Homecoming videos and sings on the Homecoming tour. In addition, Ivan has a solo concert ministry.

The SGMA honored Ivan as Soloist of the Year in 1998. He has been voted Favorite Lead Vocalist six times and Favorite Male Vocalist eight times by *Singing News*. In 2001, 2002, 2003, and 2004, *Singing News* fans voted Ivan Soloist of the Year.

Ivan and his wife, Teresa, have two sons, Ryan and Josh.

Squire Parsons

April 4, 1948—

Thou shalt no more be termed Forsaken; neither shall thy land any more be termed Desolate: but thou shalt be called Hephzibah, and thy land Beulah: for the LORD delighteth in thee, and thy land shall be married. Isaiah 62:4

Squire Enos Parsons, Jr., was born in Newton, West Virginia. He and his wife, Linda, live in Leicester, North Carolina, and have four children. Squire bears the family name that goes back as far as his great-grandfather, Squire Smith. He grew up singing gospel music at home and at church where Squire, Sr. was the music leader. His mother influenced his musical inclinations as she played 78-rpm recordings of the Statesmen, the Blackwood Brothers, and the Chuck Wagon Gang. Wonderful family music continuously surrounded him at home on the mountain farm in West Virginia. Family gatherings included singing from music in the shaped-note style, which Squire, Sr. taught locally.

Through the years Squire's love of gospel music continued to grow. He studied music, received a bachelor of science in music education, and taught music in public schools. At the same time, he sang with the Calvarymen and then joined the Kingsmen Quartet of Asheville, North Carolina, in 1975. Squire left the Kingsmen in 1979 to start the solo ministry in which he is still active today.

Squire has been active both performing and composing gospel music. His most popular song, "Sweet Beulah Land," was released in 1979 on his first solo recording. It was voted Song of the Year in 1981 by *Singing News* magazine. Other popular songs recorded by Squire include "He Came to Me" and "Broken Rose."

Squire often expresses the desire that when the people "leave our concerts, they will be saying, 'Oh, what a Savior' rather than 'Oh, what a singer.'"

—*Nancy Gossett*

Janet Paschal

O LORD, you have searched me and you know me. You know when
I sit and when I rise; you perceive my thoughts from afar.
Psalm 139:1–2 NIV

orn in Reidsville, North Carolina, Janet Ann Paschal grew up listening to Judy Garland and Barbra Streisand. She was also influenced by her family's passion for music, often through her father and uncles' group, the Paschal Brothers. After graduating from high school and as her desire to sing escalated, Janet began to pursue her dream to sing professionally.

Janet joined the Rex Nelon Singers, where her powerful soprano vocals became a benchmark of excellence in the gospel music world. She was greatly inspired by Rex's leadership, and she enjoyed many successes with the group.

Janet later expanded her interests, recording her first solo album in 1988 and embarking on a solo career. From national television appearances to becoming a mainstay on the Gaither Homecoming Concert Series around the world, Janet's smile and her profound ability to "vividly bring a song to life onstage" have inspired countless people.

Janet has enjoyed two Grammy nominations, three Dove nominations, and has been lauded in several top female vocalist categories in the industry. Her performances and songwriting talents range from a national ceremony at the Tomb of the Unknown Soldier in Washington, D.C., to appearances alongside Billy Graham.

Janet is also known for her search for truth in life captured in her journal writings. She collected these poetic inspirations from her personal journey into a book, *The Good Road.* In 1992 part of that journey led Janet to become the official spokesperson for Mission of Mercy, an international Christian relief organization.

In 1999 Janet married commercial airline pilot, John Lanier. The two make their home in her native North Carolina.

—Celeste Winstead

Sandi Patty

July 12, 1956—

Then said Jesus to those Jews which believed on him, If ye continue in my word, then are ye my disciples indeed; And ye shall know the truth, and the truth shall make you free. John 8:31–32.

andra Faye Patty was only two years old when she sang her first solo. The place was the church in Oklahoma City, Oklahoma, where her father, Ron, was minister of music and her mother, Carolyn, was the church pianist. Sandi remembers growing up in church and says that she and her two younger brothers had to "sit on the front row, right in front of the piano, so my mom could keep an eye on us."

As one of the most highly acclaimed performers in our time, Sandi has received thirty-nine Dove Awards, five Grammy Awards, four *Billboard* Music Awards, and is a 2004 inductee into the GMA Gospel Music Hall of Fame. This recognition makes her the most awarded female vocalist in contemporary Christian music history. Her three platinum and five gold albums have sold more than eleven million copies.

Sandi was introduced to the nation in 1986 during the rededication of the Statue of Liberty when her rendition of "The Star Spangled Banner" was broadcast on ABC's *Liberty Weekend* special.

In the early days of her career, more than two decades ago, Sandi traveled extensively with the Bill Gaither Trio. It was there that she learned some invaluable lessons about the importance of recreating feelings for the audience.

Today, Sandi says that she is honored, humbled, and grateful to sing in congregations across the country. She further declares, "If I can encourage people in their journey with Christ, if I can challenge them to draw closer to the Lord, *that* is what I want my music to do."

Glen Payne

October 20, 1926—October 15, 1999

And we know that all things work together for good to them that love God, to them who are the called according to his purpose. Romans 8:28

len Weldon Payne was born in Royse City, Texas. When he was seven, his grandfather took him to hear V. O. Stamps and his quartet, an unforgettable experience for Glen. He knew then what he wanted to do with his life. Beginning in 1939 he attended the Stamps School of Music for four years. The fundamentals he learned there laid the foundation for a career that lasted nearly sixty years.

After a stint in the army, Glen returned to teach in the Stamps School of Music. While there, he sang with two quartets, the Frank Stamps Quartet and the Stamps-Ozark Quartet. In January 1957 he joined the Weatherfords. Then, in August 1963 Glen formed a trio to sing for the Cathedral of Tomorrow in Akron, Ohio. Members of the trio included Bobby Clark and Danny Coker. After a year and a half, the trio became a quartet. Eventually, Glen co-owned the quartet with George Younce and also served as the manager. The Cathedral Quartet became known as the premier group in southern gospel music.

At the Cathedral of Tomorrow Glen met Van Harris, whom he married on November 30, 1958. Glen and Van became the parents of Carla, Todd, and Darla and grandparents of Jordan, Marla, and Cole.

Over his lifetime in gospel music, Glen was nominated for eleven Grammys. As a member of the Cathedrals, he was inducted into the Gospel Music Association Hall of Fame, the Texas Music Hall of Fame, the Southern Gospel Music Hall of Fame, and the Radio Music Hall of Fame.

Guy Penrod

July 2, 1963—

For even the Son of man came not to be ministered unto, but to minister, and to give his life a ransom for many. Mark 10:45

uy Penrod claims Abilene, Texas, as his hometown. His father was a preacher in New Mexico where, at the age of three, Guy sang his first solo, "Fill My Cup, Lord." Guy remembers the church being the focus of Penrod family life, but he never really dreamed of being a musician.

Guy has a bachelor of arts degree in music from Liberty University where he attended on a music scholarship and sang with a traveling group that accompanied Jerry Falwell on his engagements.

A fellow Liberty student became his wife on the evening of his graduation day. Guy's first position after graduation was teaching music in a junior high school in Atlanta. He says that it was a good experience but one for which he would not volunteer again.

After a move to Nashville, Guy began doing session work, singing jingles, and appearing in TNN's "Music City Tonight." He has provided backup vocals for such artists as Amy Grant, Michael W. Smith, Larnelle Harris, Garth Brooks, James Ingram, Steve Green, and Phillips, Craig, and Dean. He also made appearances with the Gaither Vocal Band.

Then came a call from Bill Gaither stating that the Vocal Band was looking for a lead singer. In the spring of 1994 after a decade of singing backup for others, Guy took the lead in one of the industry's most celebrated groups.

Guy says the Vocal Band is family friendly, which grants him "daddy time" with his boys. According to Guy, his wife, Angie, is a lifelong student and homeschools their seven sons, Tyler, Logan, Joe, Jesse, Levi, Grayson, and Zechariah. The family enjoys hiking in the woods and riding horses.

David Phelps

October 21, 1969—

The LORD is my shepherd; I shall not want . . . Psalm 23

orn in Dallas, Texas, David Norris Phelps grew up in Temball, where his unusual singing talent was recognized. David knew he wanted to perform music for the glory of God, but in college David was encouraged to sing opera or to sing on Broadway. However, his love for Christian music outweighed all other options. In 1988 while he was still in his teens, David became the youngest winner of the Seminar in the Rockies held in Estes Park, Colorado. After graduation from high school, he was the artist-in-residence for a church in Hurst, Texas.

In 1996 David and his wife, Lori, packed up their earthly belongings and headed to Nashville to fulfill his dream of becoming a Christian artist. After six months with no job offers and their funds getting low, they made a weekend trip back to Texas. While David and Lori were there, his family prayed for a miracle. When they returned to Nashville the next day, God answered the prayers. David heard about an opportunity with the Gaither Vocal Band and officially became a member two weeks later.

With the Gaither Vocal Band, David has received four Dove Awards and two Grammy Awards. He recently began a solo career and released a solo project called *Revelation* with songs that he wrote or co-wrote. David especially likes the first line of "Break Free" which says: "Forget what you've heard about Jesus if it doesn't begin and end with love."

David says he is unable to choose a favorite song because he has so many. He is living his dream and reaching thousands of people with his wonderful tenor voice. Lori reminds him to honor God who gave him the talent. He and Lori have four children, Callie, Maggie, Grant, and Coby.

Rosa Nell Speer Powell

September 21, 1922—

The LORD is my shepherd; I shall not want . . . Psalm 23

Born in Double Springs, Alabama, Rosa Nell was the second child of Tom and Lena Speer. "Rosie" followed in the footsteps of her older brother, Brock.

The story goes that as soon as the children were talking, their father made sure they were on pitch. The Speer Family consisted of Tom ("Dad") and Lena ("Mom") and Tom's sister and brother-in-law, Pearl and Logan Claborn. Since the group needed accompaniment for the singers, each child was given an instrument to play. Rosie was given the piano, and she has delighted audiences ever since with her unique style of playing.

When Dad Speer took a job with the Vaughn Music Company, the family moved to Lawrenceburg, Tennessee. To further their music career, Dad Speer felt the family should move to Nashville in 1946. It wasn't long before Rosie met James Edwin Powell; they were married on June 19, 1948. For the first time, a family member left the group.

Rosie and Edwin started the Powell Lacey Quartet. They appeared in churches and concerts and had their own radio program broadcasting from Sand Mountain, Alabama. Besides rearing three children and two stepchildren, Rosa Nell taught piano lessons; she is still teaching young people to play.

After Edwin's death in 1979, Rosa Nell and Mary Tom, also a widow, rejoined the Speers. Once again Rosie's piano playing was memorable. The Alabama Music Hall of Fame recognized her contribution to the Speer Family. Although Rosie is now retired, she has appeared on several Gaither Homecoming videos.

—Faye Speer

Elvis Presley

January 8, 1935–August 16, 1977

Delight thyself also in the LORD; and he shall give thee the desires of thine heart. Psalm 37:4

lvis Aron Presley was born in humble surroundings in Tupelo, Mississippi, to Vernon and Gladys Presley. Hoping for a better life, the family moved to Memphis where they attended the Assembly of God church. In church Elvis developed the love for gospel music that profoundly affected his singing style.

Elvis was particularly fond of the Blackwood Brothers Quartet and the Statesmen. The Stamps and the Imperials, two groups Elvis frequently sang with, were organized respectively by J. D. Sumner of the Blackwood Brothers and Jake Hess of the Statesmen.

Elvis's association with gospel music stretched from the beginning to the end of his career. At Elvis's first recording session in Nashville, Ben and Brock Speer, along with Gordon Stoker of the Jordanaires, sang backup. After he became the most successful artist in the world he continued to show up at all-night gospel sings. He often invited the quartets to perform with him on his tours; and, after the shows, he would ask the musicians back to his suite to sing gospel music. That was when Elvis's fun began, remembered former Imperial Joe Moscheo.

Elvis had fourteen Grammy nominations. His three wins were for his gospel recordings: *How Great Thou Art* in 1967, *He Touched Me* in 1972, and his live Memphis recording of the song "How Great Thou Art" in 1974. Elvis's love of gospel music is apparent on the video, *He Touched Me: The Gospel Music of Elvis Presley:* Introducing J. D. Sumner and the Stamps to sing "Sweet, Sweet Spirit," he stands quietly listening with tears streaming down his face. The new recording by the Stamps was on Elvis's record player the day he died.

Millions of recordings were sold during Elvis's lifetime, and since then sales have soared past the one billion mark. In 2001 Elvis was inducted posthumously into the GMA Gospel Music Hall of Fame. Priscilla Presley states in *Elvis by the Presleys,* "Gospel music was his deepest roots and, I believe, his deepest love." —*Judy Spencer Nelon*

Wesley Pritchard

February 9, 1961—

Those things, which ye have both learned, and received, and heard, and seen in me, do: and the God of peace shall be with you.
Philippians 4:9

evin Wesley Pritchard was born in Lenoir, North Carolina, and grew up in a pastor's home. Wesley says, "I never knew anything else but singing. My family has been singing all my life." A producer, arranger, and singer in the 1980s, Wesley toured with Higher Ground and Michael W. Smith. He uses his expertise in these areas at Mill West Studios, the recording studio he owns with Milton Smith.

Wesley's first solo album, *Champion of Love*, was released in 2002. The project has old favorites, some new songs, and a couple of songs that Wesley and his wife, Teresa, co-wrote. For two years Wesley sang with the Old Friends Quartet, which included Ernie Haase and gospel legends George Younce and Jake Hess. The quartet's first project, *Encore*, earned Wesley his first Dove Award in 2002 for Southern Gospel Album of the Year. Wesley says, "This project was one of the greatest things I have ever been involved with." Old Friends Quartet released another album, *Feelin' Fine*, in 2003.

Wesley lives in Fayetteville, North Carolina, with his wife, Teresa. They have two children: Erica, who is a speech pathologist assistant, and Kramer, who is studying recording technologies at Barton College.

Wesley is the worship leader at Fayetteville Community Church where he and his father are co-pastors.

Wesley's favorite song is "Going Home."

Dottie Rambo

Neglect not the gift that is in thee, which was given thee by prophecy, with the laying on of the hands of the presbytery. 1 Timothy 4:14

nown as "Dottie," Joyce Reba Rambo was born in Madisonville, Kentucky, and grew up in Morganfield, Kentucky. She wrote her first song at the age of eight. Even though she was a fan of the Grand Ole Opry, she couldn't know that one day she would perform there and that her songs would be heard around the world.

Dottie left home at the age of twelve to enter a full-time career of singing and composing music. She married at the age of sixteen and became a mother at eighteen. Her family became the Rambos, known worldwide for their distinct, award-winning harmonies that set precedents in the gospel music world. Dottie penned such classics as "We Shall Behold Him," "If That Isn't Love," "The Perfect Rose," "Behold the Lamb," and countless others.

Dottie has won a Grammy, the ASCAP Lifetime Achievement Award, Dove Awards, and Christian Country Music Association Awards. She has been inducted into the GMA Gospel Music Hall of Fame and the SGMA Hall of Fame, in addition to being named Songwriter of the Century.

Dottie testifies, "I grew up in a family of eleven children. My older sister, Nellie, is like a mother to me; and of course, we were always close to our mother. My father was very abusive and asked me to leave home when I was twelve because I wanted to be a gospel singer. So I left. The rest is history. Later, when he was on his deathbed, I led my father to the Lord; and he was my best friend. God has brought me through so much. God sent me a new anointing and touched me in a very special way."

—*Celeste Winstead*

Lynda Randle

February 7, 1962—

For the LORD God is a sun and shield: the LORD will give grace and glory: no good thing will he withhold from them that walk uprightly. Psalm 84:11

Born and reared in the inner-city culture of Washington, D.C., Lynda Randle has used her early experiences to bring depth to her ministry. The middle child of seven in a family of singers, Lynda wanted to be a cosmetologist. Her father, a part-time pastor who has had a great influence on her life, led her to a relationship with the Lord when she was twelve. According to Lynda, her singing mother was her first Mahalia Jackson.

In the ninth grade Lynda was sent to a Christian school. There in suburban Maryland, she joined an all-white choir where she truly found her voice and began entering and winning regional competitions. After winning the Mahalia Jackson Award in D.C. at eighteen, Lynda was offered a music scholarship to Liberty University. When she sang at various events, she always asked her audiences to pray for her, because she wanted to be the world's greatest gospel singer. In 1981 God helped her realize that her personal goal was not as important as the fact that she had His anointing.

Lynda's concert work led her to Kansas City and a youth minister, Michael Randle. She was singing on local television where Michael happened to see her. They were married two years later. At a women's conference just before her marriage, Lynda met Gloria Gaither, who invited her to videotapings and to join the Homecoming Friends in concerts. Lynda has also been following her lifelong dream of speaking at women's conferences.

Lynda and Michael have two daughters, Patience and Joy. The girls are homeschooled, which allows the family to travel together to Lynda's concerts. Her deep, rich voice is born out of experience and wisdom beyond her years.

Naomi Sego Reader

February 17, 1931—

For God so loved the world, that he gave his only begotten Son, that whosoever believeth in him should not perish, but have everlasting life. John 3:16

Born in Enigma, Georgia, Ruth Naomi Easters is one of five ladies credited with being the "first ladies" of gospel music. In 1949 Naomi married James Sego, and the couple moved to Macon, Georgia. James had a gospel group named the Harmony Kings that later changed its name to the Sego Brothers Quartet. During the late 1950s the Quartet sang live every Saturday on WMAZ-TV in Macon. One day when a singer was ill, James asked Naomi if she wanted to sing on television that day. She did and the station was flooded with calls. Naomi became a permanent member, and the group became the Sego Brothers and Naomi.

In 1958 the Sego Brothers and Naomi became known worldwide when they recorded their first album with the hit song, "Is My Lord Satisfied with Me?" In 1962 through the success of the song, "Sorry, I Never Knew You," they became the first group in the history of gospel music to have a million-selling record.

The group continued to tour and record throughout the 1960s and 1970s until James passed away in the late 1970s. Naomi continued the ministry after James' death. When she married evangelist Vernon Reader, the group name changed again—this time to Naomi and the Segos.

Well into her fourth decade of singing gospel music, Naomi continues to tour. In 2001 she was inducted into the SGMA Hall of Fame. She makes regular appearances on Homecoming videos and is more in demand than ever.

Don Reid

June 5, 1945—

Wisdom is the principal thing; therefore get wisdom: and with all thy getting get understanding. Proverbs 4:7

B orn and reared in Staunton, Virginia, Donald Sidney Reid is the spokesman for the Statlers and is their primary songwriter. During times of contemplation, Don has written such favorites as "Class of '57" and "Do You Know You Are My Sunshine?" He claims the Blackwood Brothers and the Statesmen Quartet as his musical influences.

The Statler Brothers, which also includes Phil Balsley, Jimmy Fortune, and Don's brother, Harold, have received over 500 awards in their forty years of entertaining, including three Grammy awards and nine Country Music Association Awards. Many folks will remember their highly rated television show on TNN in the early 1990s. The Statler Brothers placed second, just behind Frank Sinatra, in the 1996 National Harris Poll taken to determine America's favorite singers.

Don says, "I grew up in the Presbyterian church, not a usual denomination for giving root to loving southern gospel music. I was baptized there as a babe in arms and never missed a Sunday. Traveling the country music circuit for most of my life, I tried never to miss a Sunday, even on the road. I never had a 'Damascus Road' experience but have always been a Christian—a better one at times than at others. Today I'm an elder in the church I grew up in and so are both of my sons. This one fact gives me more joy than maybe anything else in my life."

Since he retired from traveling, Don has written two books, *Heroes and Outlaws of the Bible* and *Sunday Morning Memories*. Don is married to Deborah and has two sons, Debo and Langdon.

Harold Reid

August 21, 1939—

For God so loved the world, that he gave his only begotten Son, that whosoever believeth in him should not perish, but have everlasting life. John 3:16

Harold Wilson Reid was born in Augusta County, Virginia, and reared in Staunton. Known as the clown of the Statler Brothers, he claims in all seriousness that the name of the group was taken from a box of tissues in a hotel room and "could just as easily have been the Kleenex Brothers."

Harold and his brother, Don, were the writers for the Statler Brothers Show. Harold supervised all their album covers and coordinated their bookings. The Statlers have recorded fifty albums and have earned thirteen gold and eight platinum albums.

Harold's musical influences began with the singing cowboys: Roy Rogers, Gene Autry, and Tex Ritter. Southern gospel quartets known as the Blackwood Brothers and the Statesmen Quartet came along later. He was greatly encouraged and impressed by his high school choir director, George Sargent. Also influential were Bing Crosby, Dean Martin, and Tennessee Ernie Ford, but Harold always came back to southern gospel music. He declares, "To this day there is still more talent buried in that industry than is evident in any other."

Harold also confides, "I truly and honestly think I've always been a member of the flock, maybe not always in good standing, but never a lost sheep. I have strayed, but never been lost. There was always church, family, friends, and heroes that never let go of me. I've always been one of those very fortunate individuals who can take the word of the wise that the stove is hot. I don't have to touch it. I can look at the destruction and desperation of other people and learn by their mistakes. God has been good to me. I have a wonderful life and look forward to a heavenly reward that I don't deserve, but through the love of God and the blood of the Son, I have been promised."

Harold and his wife, Brenda, have five children, Kim, Karman, Kodi, Kasey, and Wil.

Mary Tom Speer Reid

June 13, 1925—

For God so loved the world, that he gave his only begotten Son, that whosoever believeth in him should not perish, but have everlasting life. John 3:16

ary Tom Speer was born in Double Springs, Alabama, the third child of Tom and Lena Speer. In 1930 the family moved to Lawrenceburg, Tennessee, so their father could sing for the Vaughn Music Company. Family singing was relegated to weekends because Tom felt very strongly that children should be in school during the week, not traveling.

The family's next move took them to Montgomery, Alabama, for a radio show. Then, in 1946 the family moved to Nashville so that sons Brock and Ben could attend Trevecca Nazarene University.

During a musical event Mary Tom met a Trevecca student and radio announcer. After a few dates she became Mrs. Robert L. Reid on April 30, 1954. As the original alto of the Speer Family, Mary Tom continued to sing with the group until Bob finished seminary. He was a pastor in the Lutheran Church of America until he passed away in December 1968.

Mary Tom has worked as the secretary for Ben Speer Publishing Company since 1969 and keeps things organized for the Ben Speer Stamps-Baxter School of Music. At the school where she serves as dorm mother, students love and adore her.

Mary Tom is the mother of three children, Teri, Cyndi, and Timothy, and grandmother of six. She continues to play the piano for her Sunday school class and usually has a solo ready to sing.

Mary Tom has been featured often on Gaither Homecoming videos. Bill Gaither remarks that he has received many comments about Mary Tom's smile and pleasantness.

As a member of the First Family of Gospel Music, Mary Tom still performs admirably with the best of vocalists. She has been inducted into the Alabama Music Hall of Fame.

—*Faye Speer*

Tim Riley

August 29, 1945—

But seek first his kingdom and his righteousness, and all these things will be given to you as well. Matthew 6:33 NIV

L oyd Riley sang bass with the Stamps-Baxter Quartet. When he married Eva, little did he know that their son, Tim, would one day sing bass and lead his own award-winning quartet, Gold City. Loyd was minister of music during Tim's formative years at the Baptist Church in Glencoe, Alabama. Tim loved music, and when he was three, he would play on the family's pump organ the songs he had heard at church. When Tim's dad suggested that he sing with the FFA Quartet, he didn't really want to at the time. However, the love of singing quartet-style music soon started burning within, and he says, "from that day on I had to do it."

The path to the top was not easy. Tim credits his success to many folks who helped and encouraged him when he was struggling to launch a career and support his family. Tim singles out his dear friend, Rex Nelon, for special thanks, because Rex gave Tim the opportunity to sing by providing him with a job selling music.

For a time Tim sang with the Southmen Quartet and even now continues to celebrate at the annual Homecoming Concert with friends from this era: Jack Toney, Larry Beck, and Jim Hefner. Tim's Gold City Quartet launched the careers of Brian Free, Ivan Parker, Mike Le Fevre, and Garry Jones.

Today Tim is happy to stay home more and enjoy time with his wife, Barbara, his grandchildren, and his daughter, Amy. His sons, Doug and Danny, are carrying on the family music tradition with Gold City. Tim is proud of Doug's arranging, producing, and playing drums and of Danny's singing and managing Gold City. Tim says, "Danny has the same fire burning in his bones as his daddy." —*Judy Spencer Nelon*

Charlotte Penhollow Ritchie

June 23, 1974—

A good name is rather to be chosen than great riches, and loving favour rather than silver and gold. . . . By humility and the fear of the LORD *are riches, and honour, and life.* Proverbs 22:1, 4

Born in Havre de Grace, Maryland, Charlotte Marie Penhollow considers her family special beyond words. Her parents married at a young age and gave birth to her brother, Ronnie, within two years of marriage. Eleven years later Charlotte was born, followed four years later by her brother, Jonathan. Despite the age gaps, the siblings are very close.

"My parents tried to spend quality time with us, making memories that would last," she explains. "My dad loves music and has been singing for as long as I can remember, and my mom is very creative. We didn't have a lot growing up, but we were loved."

Charlotte was influenced musically by her dad, Allen Penhollow, Cynthia Clawson, the Eagles, Céline Dion, Martina McBride, and Sandi Patty. Her inspiring soprano vocals opened the opportunity to join the Nelons. In 1995 Jeff Easter introduced Charlotte to Greg Ritchie, the drummer for Jeff and Sheri Easter, at a Homecoming videotaping. Within a year, Charlotte and Greg were married; soon afterwards, Charlotte began singing with the Easters.

Whether singing onstage nightly with Jeff and Sheri, on the Homecoming stage with numerous other artists, or in the studios of Nashville, Charlotte's voice has become one of the most distinctive and soothing sounds in the industry. She is known for her rendition of "Go Rest High on That Mountain" and has been nominated numerous times for Soprano of the Year. Her favorite song is "Love of God."

Charlotte and Greg make their home in Lincolnton, Georgia, and have a son, Landon, who travels with them on the bus with Jeff and Sheri Easter.

—Celeste Winstead

239

Rosie Rozell

August 29, 1928—February 28, 1995

But seek first his kingdom and his righteousness, and all these things will be given to you as well. Matthew 6:33 NIV

oland Dwayne "Rosie" Rozell was born in Hardy, Oklahoma, and became one of the premier tenors in southern gospel music. Rosie began his career with the Tulsa Trumpeteers in the mid-1950s. He attracted the attention of the Statesmen while they were touring in the area, and the group hired him in 1958. To his singing Rosie brought emotion and soul that other tenors lacked. His rendition of "What a Savior!" became a gospel classic, and he thrilled audiences with his performances of "Hide Thou Me" and "Leave It There."

During his decade and a half with the Statesmen, Rosie helped the group remain at the top of the gospel music charts. He left the Statesmen in 1970 to form a new group known as Rosie Rozell and the Searchers. This group included Rosie's wife, Betty, and friends, Jack Toney, Mildred and Nelson LeCroy, and John and Sandy Payton. At a time when using an organ was unique for a gospel quartet, they took a Hammond organ on the road, and both Betty and Sandy played it in concerts.

Rosie later enjoyed home life with his wife and their son, Marty, when they became church musicians. He returned to the Statesmen for a brief period in the mid-1970s.

In 1981 Rosie joined Jake Hess, Hovie Lister, J. D. Sumner, and James Blackwood as a founding member of the Masters V. However, health problems soon forced Rosie to leave the road. For twenty years he had been one of the most popular figures in gospel music. Despite poor health, his performances retained an amazing quality and consistency.

Rosie passed away in 1995; in 1999 he was inducted posthumously into the Southern Gospel Music Association Hall of Fame.

Bill Shaw

June 22, 1924—

He put a new song in my mouth, a hymn of praise to our God. Many will see and fear and put their trust in the LORD. Psalm 40:3 NIV

ill was born Edward Lamar Shaw in Lowndesville, South Carolina, not far from the Georgia state line. His mother, Minnie, and father, Edward, moved to Anderson, South Carolina, while Bill was a baby. Liking the song "Billy Boy" so much, Bill's aunt started calling her nephew "Billy." The name stuck.

Without formal training Bill started playing the bass fiddle and singing with his brothers-in-law, Walker and Jimmy Pickens, in churches in the area. In 1949 Bill joined a men's choral group led by John Townsend and was encouraged to study voice and read musical notation. Later that year, he began singing with the Harmo-Knights Quartet.

Early in 1952 Bill joined the South Land Quartet, and from April until September of 1952 he sang with the All American Quartet. Bill joined the Blackwood Brothers in September 1952. While he was with them, they won six Grammy Awards. He left the group in October 1973. Bill has composed several songs including: "Because of the Love of the Lord for Me," "I'm Thankful," "My Lord Goes with Me," "The Way Is the Way of the Cross," and his most-requested song, "Pablo."

Bill was crowned "King of Gospel Singers" in 1958 and in 1998 recorded a CD entitled, *Bill Shaw's Gospel Favorites.*

Bill married Wilma Pickens in 1950. They have four children, Susan, Steve, Bob, and Lori, and seven grandchildren.

Hazel Slaughter

__May 29, 1935—__

And we know that all things work together for good to them that love God, to them who are the called according to his purpose. Romans 8:28

orn in Meridian, Mississippi, Hazel Myers grew up in Laurel, receiving the legacy of music and singing from her mother, Lena. Hazel grew up singing in church and participated in special singing ensembles throughout her high school years.

Hazel met Henry Slaughter in Laurel when he and an evangelist came to her church for a summer revival series and they soon believed they were meant to sing duets together. Even before they were married, Hazel and Henry knew the Lord had something special in music ministry for them.

They sang their songs in local churches for the first eight years of their marriage. In the early 1960s they became part of the music ministry of the Cathedral of Tomorrow. Hazel remembers, "Neither of us ever planned to have such a ministry that developed over the years. We just simply followed the Lord as He opened the doors of opportunity to us."

After more than four decades of gospel music ministry, the Slaughters have reached into all parts of the country. Still being in demand nationally by an assorted group of churches testifies to their strong influence on lives wherever and whenever they are heard.

They have recorded over twenty-four albums, have received five Dove Awards, and for seven years traveled with the Bill Gaither Trio.

Hazel and Henry are the parents of two sons, David and Michael, and a daughter, Amanda. "Great Is Thy Faithfulness" is Hazel's favorite song.

All their deserved recognition and awards fade in comparison to their current testimony and music, ushering in a fresh flow of God's Spirit in His people.

Henry Slaughter

January 9, 1927—

But seek ye first the kingdom of God, and his righteousness; and all these things shall be added unto you. Matthew 6:33

enry Thaxton Slaughter was born in Roxboro, North Carolina, his middle name coming from the doctor who delivered him. Henry's father, M. T., came from a musical family. Because he was frail as a child, Henry's mother Lila encouraged him to take piano lessons and to try to excel in this area. He remembers his piano teacher, Mrs. Newell, and the beginnings of his love for classical music. His other musical influences came from the Oak Grove Baptist Church in Roxboro, North Carolina.

By the age of twenty Henry had begun playing for the Stamps-Ozark Quartet. He again played for them in 1955 and 1956 and for the Tulsa Trumpeteers in 1956 and 1957. He later accompanied the Weatherford Quartet for three years. In 1963 Henry became one of the original members of the Imperials.

Henry met Hazel when he came to her church for a summer revival service. They were married on December 20, 1952. In the early 1960s Henry and Hazel were part of the ministry at the Cathedral of Tomorrow in Akron, Ohio. From 1969 to 1976 Henry and Hazel traveled with the Bill Gaither Trio during taping sessions.

Henry has numerous compositions to his credit, including "What a Precious Friend Is He," "If the Lord Wasn't Walking by My Side," and "Then the Answer Came."

Henry received five Dove Awards for Best Gospel Instrumentalist of the Year in the 1970s. His favorite song is "Great Is Thy Faithfulness."

Henry and Hazel have three children, David, Michael, and Amanda.

Ladye Love Smith

June 5, 1964—

I can do all things through Christ which strengtheneth me.
Philippians 4:13

L adye Love Long was born in Memphis but grew up in Iuka, Mississippi. She was saved during a revival at age seven and recognizes that music played a part in her coming to know Christ. In the Baptist church where she grew up, there was a wonderful youth choir and a band that traveled and recorded records. Their minister of music was a converted Jew. Since Ladye Love's older sisters and brother were in the choir, she couldn't wait to be in it, too. As she watched and listened, she realized there was more to it than the music, and she began hearing God's promises. She wanted that, too! She walked the aisle and prayed to ask Christ to come into her heart. Her pastor asked to meet with her the next week to make sure she really understood her action. Later she was baptized.

Ladye graduated from the University of Mississippi with a vocal performance major, a radio and television minor, and then earned a master's degree in counseling. While living in Orlando, Florida, she sang at Disney's Epcot Center in Voices of Liberty. She has also been a backup singer for Larnelle Harris, Sandi Patty, Lee Greenwood, and Brenda Lee.

Ladye and husband, Reggie Smith, are known internationally for their vocal expertise. They have performed in thirteen countries and in some of the most outstanding venues in the world: Super Bowl XXVI, the Kremlin, and New York City's Carnegie Hall. They have also performed for President and Mrs. Bush and for Billy Graham crusades.

In their concerts Ladye and Reggie provide far more than just entertainment. They are able also to minister to the personal concerns of the people in attendance.

In 2004, Ladye Love and Reggie finalized the adoption of a little boy, Bret, who has been with them since he was fifteen months old.

Reggie Smith

November 29, 1965—

Let your speech be alway with grace, seasoned with salt, that ye may know how ye ought to answer every man. Colossians 4:6

eggie Smith grew up in Moselle, just outside Hattiesburg, Mississippi. His dad was an elementary school principal and for thirty-three years was minister of music in the Baptist church the family attended. Reggie's mother played the piano, and frequently Reggie and his two brothers sang. Reggie's father also farmed soybeans on the side. Reggie vividly remembers going home after school and ball practice and heading straight to the fields to the tractor, where he also spent his summers. To this day he loves the country and its simplicity.

While growing up, Reggie had two loves, music and sports. He played in the band and was on the football team. When he had to choose between the two, he chose football. He played college football at Jones Junior College and later attended Delta State University on a music and football scholarship. When he transferred to the University of Mississippi, he met Ladye Love Long. Both of them toured throughout the United States and Europe with Concert Singers. Reggie also sang during college with Selah. His brother, a cousin, and a friend were a part of this group.

While living in Orlando, Florida, Reggie sang for Universal Studios and Disney, including vocals on *The Lion King* soundtrack. He has traveled with Larnelle Harris and others.

After a move to Nashville, Reggie and his best friend, Ladye Love, began dating. They were married in 1995 and adopted a son, Bret, in 2004.

Today Reggie participates in Gaither Homecoming Concerts, as well as in concerts with Ladye. Reggie is a session singer and owns a recording studio in Nashville, Reggie's Attic, where he produces music for many artists and groups.

Ben Speer

June 26, 1930—

And we know that all things work together for good to them that love God, to them who are the called according to his purpose. Romans 8:28

B en Lacey Speer was the youngest child born to Tom and Lena Speer. Along with the rest of the children, he was born in Double Springs, Alabama. When he was a child, Ben showed off his musical talent by playing a ukulele and by standing on the end of the piano bench playing and singing.

The family moved to Lawrenceburg, Tennessee, so that his dad could write songs and sing with the Vaughn Quartet. An offer for a radio program required the family to move to Montgomery, Alabama, where their music was available to more people. In 1946 the family moved to Nashville so that Ben and his brother Brock could continue their education.

In 1953 Ben married Mildred Bradley. They have three children, Stephen, Lisa, and Darien, and are now the proud grandparents of five. Ben sang with the family group all over Canada, the United States, and Europe. In 1993 he resigned from the Speer Family but not from gospel music. For the past fifteen years he has been producing the Homeland EZ Key Soundtracks, recording five songs a month. He manages Welcome Home Records and owns his studio in Nashville. Ben's publishing company has published such hits as "What a Day That Will Be," "I'm Standing on the Solid Rock," and "I'll Walk Them Golden Stairs." The latter was recorded by Elvis Presley. Ben also leads the Stamps-Baxter School of Music in Nashville, where he teaches young and old the unique genre of southern gospel music.

Ben was inducted into the GMA Gospel Music Hall of Fame in 1995, into the SGMA Hall of Fame in 1998, into the Alabama Hall of Fame, and is a director for the National Quartet Convention. At present Ben is music director for the Gaither Homecoming Video Series and travels with Gaither Homecoming Concerts.
—*Faye Speer*

Brock Speer

December 28, 1920—March 29, 1999

He that dwelleth in the secret place of the most High shall abide under the shadow of the Almighty. Psalm 91:1

Jackson Brock Speer was born in Winston County, Alabama, just two months before his father and mother began a singing group called the Speer Quartet. For the remaining seventy-eight years of his life, he was inextricably intertwined with that group. With only one interruption—World War II—he sang with his family his entire life. When the Speer Quartet began its career, it traveled by horse and buggy, moved up to a Model T Ford and later to a customized bus, traveling over 100,000 miles annually until retirement in 1998.

Brock sang to crowds as large as 200,000 at Explo '72, to church congregations of less than a hundred, to President Jimmy Carter on the White House lawn, and to untold millions over radio, television, and through recordings. His group recorded some seventy albums, won fourteen Dove Awards, and received seven Grammy nominations.

A 1950 graduate of Trevecca College with a bachelor's degree in theology, Brock also earned a master of divinity from Vanderbilt University. In 1997 he was recognized with an honorary doctorate of music by Trevecca Nazarene University.

In 1998 the Speers were inducted into the GMA Gospel Music Hall of Fame, the first year groups were included. They were the only group ever to receive the GMA Lifetime Achievement Award. Brock was past president, chairman of the board, and a permanent board member of the Gospel Music Association.

Beyond all that, Brock was married to his "darling wife Faye" for fifty years and earned the love and fierce devotion of his children, Suzan, Marc, and Brian.

These words are a portion of those written by Brock's nephew, Steve Speer, and first appeared in Brock's funeral bulletin, April 1, 1999.

Faye Speer

October 19, 1928—

Likewise the Spirit also helpeth our infirmities: for we know not what we should pray for as we ought: but the Spirit itself maketh intercession for us with groanings which cannot be uttered. And he that searcheth the hearts knoweth what is the mind of the Spirit, because he maketh intercession for the saints according to the will of God. Romans 8:26–27

F aye Ihrig Speer was born in Augusta, Kentucky, the daughter of a Nazarene preacher and his wife. Her parents provided a strong Christian foundation and taught her the importance of family, hard work, sacrifice, and honesty. These basic principles developed into a practical, no-nonsense approach to living for Faye. She says, "Two things I've learned in life are that God never fails and we all go through changes"—plain talk from a woman who experienced both good and sad changes in life and recognized that the steady hand of God is always near.

Faye was in her sophomore year in college, singing alto in a girl's trio, when she first laid eyes on Brock Speer. She says, "I knew he was the one for me. We fell in love and married—then my life really shifted into high gear!" The honeymoon was designed quartet style: With family in tow they headed to perform at an all-night singing.

Faye sang with the group until their children, Suzan, Marc, and Brian, came along. In the 1960s she returned to the group when Dad and Mom Speer's health began to falter. During this time she was able to complete her bachelor of science degree at Trevecca Nazarene University.

"My relationship with the Lord has been especially close since I lost Brock in 1999. I've always heard of peace that passeth all understanding, and now I know about it firsthand," confesses Faye.

The Speers have recorded seventy albums. The group and group members have won fourteen Dove Awards and have had seven Grammy nominations. Faye was recognized with a Living Legend Award from Grand Ole Gospel Reunion. She has sung many songs over the years, but her favorite is "He Is Ever Interceding."

—Suzan Speer

Lena "Mom" Speer

November 4, 1899—October 6, 1967

Fear thou not; for I am with thee: be not dismayed; for I am thy God: I will strengthen thee; yea, I will help thee; yea, I will uphold thee with the right hand of my righteousness. Isaiah 41:10

L ena Darling Brock was born in a two-room cabin at the foot of Shady Grove Hill in Cullman County, Alabama. There were two brothers and two sisters to welcome her. Since her father, Dwight Brock, was one of the county's leading musicians and music school teachers, Lena's musical education literally began in the cradle. Lena's father was an instructor for the Vaughn Music Company, and Lena often played the pump organ while he taught.

All-day singings were a favorite form of entertainment, especially in the summer. Lena's dad had a tremendous bass voice that he put to good use in the singings. One Sunday the family piled in the family wagon for a singing in Leoma, Tennessee. There, Lena met the love of her life. When Tom first heard her singing, he thought it must be the voice of an angel.

On February 27, 1920, Tom and Lena formed a beautiful duet. Lena's beautiful soprano voice added greatly to the Speer sound. Formed in 1921, the group known as the Speer Family consisted of Tom, Lena, Tom's sister, Pearl, and Pearl's husband, Logan Claborn. As soon as their children were old enough, Tom and Lena assigned them musical parts and taught them to read music. Brock, Rosa Nell, Mary Tom, and Ben soon learned that some things are not an option. You sang, and you sang it correctly. Tom had a reputation for expecting every note to be sung exactly right.

As a mixed group, the Speers have received eight Dove Awards, as well as the Gospel Music Association Lifetime Achievement Award. Lena and Tom were among the very first to be inducted into the GMA Gospel Music Hall of Fame.

Lena and Tom were pioneers in gospel music. They began a ministry that became a meaningful way to tell the story of salvation, and their message captured the hearts of those who heard it.   —*Faye Speer*

Tom "Dad" Speer

March 10, 1891—September 7, 1966

But they that wait upon the LORD shall renew their strength; they shall mount up with wings as eagles; they shall run, and not be weary; and they shall walk, and not faint. Isaiah 40:31

eorge Thomas Speer was born in Fayette County, Georgia, to a poor cotton farmer. He was the fourth child in a family that eventually numbered eighteen. Everyone worked; education was not a priority. Tom finally finished the seventh grade at the age of twenty-five. His education didn't stop there, however, because he was an avid reader of the Bible and other books that he thought worthwhile.

Tom's first musical influence came from his home. Many nights after all of the chores were finished, the family would sing around the old pump organ. People soon noticed that Tom had a special quality to his voice. In 1917 he was called for service in World War I. Since he was a lonely soldier and realized that others felt the same way he did, he soon was leading the men in singing. After spending a year in France, he arrived home and headed for an all-night singing.

On February 27, 1920, Tom married Lena Darling Brock. He liked to say, "I met a singer's daughter at a singing convention, got married in a singer's home, and raised a singing family."

Tom and Lena taught singing schools and went to singing conventions. Many times they were paid for their teaching with chickens, eggs, or whatever produce the farmers had.

Brock, Rosa Nell, Mary Tom, and Ben, their four children, formed the singing group.

In his lifetime Tom wrote over 500 songs, many of which became standards in gospel music. "Heaven's Jubilee," "Sweeter Each Day," and "Old Daniel Prayed" are just a few.

With the Speer Family, Tom Speer was inducted into the Gospel Music Association Hall of Fame.

—Faye Speer

Ira Stanphill

February 14, 1914—December 30, 1993

Jesus Christ the same yesterday, and to day, and for ever.
Hebrews 13:8

ra Forest Stanphill was born in 1914 in Belleville, New Mexico, and gave his life to the Lord when he was twelve years old. Three years later he auditioned for a radio program in Coffeyville, Kansas. Young Ira won by playing his ukulele and singing current popular songs. Ira's pastor suggested that he switch to gospel songs. The station manager agreed with the change, and Ira's program became the most popular one.

While he was still in high school, Ira wrote music and won honors in statewide competitions. He studied harmony and music composition in college and traveled with a couple of evangelists.

Ira and Gloria Holloway were married in 1951 and had daughters, Judy and Cathy. That same year MGM offered Ira a recording contract, but he chose to remain in Christian work.

John T. Benson and Pat Zondervan have published over 360 of the 500 songs that Ira wrote. In 1998 Robert Duvall sang "I Know Who Holds Tomorrow" in the movie, *The Apostle.* LeAnn Rimes sold four million copies of this song. Other favorites include "Mansion over the Hilltop," "Suppertime," "Unworthy," and "Follow Me."

A touching moment in Ira's life occurred when he visited lepers in Liberia: The lepers sang to him. Also, gospel music crossed denominational lines when Catholic nuns in Poland sang his song, "Mansion over the Hilltop."

In the late 1950s Ira sang in the Royal Albert Hall in London during the Easter season. Whether the venue was a large auditorium or a mud hut in Africa, it didn't matter to Ira who loved singing about his Savior.

⌐⌐

This biography of Ira was prepared by his wife, Gloria, for the Southern Gospel Music Association Award Banquet in 2001.

Derrell Stewart

October 12, 1934—

And we know that all things work together for good to them that love
God, to them who are the called according to his purpose. Romans 8:28

 errell Martin Stewart was born in the coastal town of Brunswick, Georgia. His father was a promoter of gospel music, and Derrell's mother encouraged him to start studying piano at the age of five. As a child Derrell didn't like to practice in front of other kids, so he had a plan: "I would run the clock up so Mama would send me to school early and I could practice before anyone got there." He learned as much as he could, and later studied under James D. Walbert in Birmingham, Alabama.

Immediately after high school, Derrell joined the Dixie Rhythm Quartet. Besides developing his unique style of playing and singing, he began wearing red socks as part of his trademark. Derrell joined the Florida Boys in February 1956. In addition to gospel, Derrell loves the big band and classical music styles.

Among other pianists, Derrell has inspired Roger Bennett and Anthony Burger. He was one of the first to receive the *Singing News* Favorite Musician Award. In 1997 he was placed on the Piano Roll of Honor at the Grand Ole Gospel Reunion. *Singing News* surprised him by having his picture on the cover of the May 2002 issue.

When he's at home, Derrell likes to play the baby grand piano his wife, Reve, gave him for Christmas one year. He and Reve enjoy scouting flea markets looking for treasures. Recently, they found an old pump organ, brought it home, cleaned it up, and polished it, and now Derrell enjoys playing it.

Derrell quips, "Reve takes good care of me and even washes my red socks every Monday." He hopes his humor and playing lift people's spirits and remind them to keep Christ in the center of their lives.

Gordon Stoker

August 3, 1924—

It is written: " 'As surely as I live,' says the Lord, 'every knee will bow before me; every tongue will confess to God.' " So then, each of us will give an account of himself to God. Romans 14:11–12 NIV

ugh Gordon Stoker was born in the small town of Gleason, Tennessee, in the telephone office building where his family made their home. His mother, Willie, was the night operator and his dad, Ambus, known locally as H. A., was the repairman. Gordon remembers being eight years old and playing an old Kimball organ for the Jolley Springs Baptist Church by the light of a coal-oil lamp. He was called Hugh Gordon and was recognized among singing circles for his talent playing piano for the Clement Trio. Mr. Clement introduced him by saying, "He's not a banker, he's not a broker, he's just the world's greatest piano player, Hugh Gordon Stoker!"

John Daniel of the Daniel Quartet was so impressed with twelve-year-old Hugh Gordon that he wanted to take him to Nashville to make him a star. For two years he appeared with the quartet on Radio WSM morning programs and the Grand Ole Opry.

After serving three years in the U.S. Army Air Corps during World War II, Gordon enrolled at Oklahoma Baptist University. In 1948 he moved back to Tennessee to continue his studies at Peabody College in Nashville. He played with the Daniel Quartet for another year until the Jordanaires came to town and he had an opportunity to join them. Shortly after that, Gordon met his future wife, as well as a young man who would change his life forever—Elvis Presley.

For over fifty years the Jordanaires have been known worldwide as one of the most versatile quartets. Their background harmony became an integral part of hit records by Elvis, Patsy Cline, and Ricky Nelson. With the Jordanaires, Gordon was inducted into the GMA Gospel Music Hall of Fame and the Country Music Hall of Fame and was awarded several Grammys.

Donnie Sumner

December 4, 1942—

*Fear thou not; for I am with thee: be not dismayed; for I am thy
God: I will strengthen thee; yea, I will help thee; yea, I will uphold
thee with the right hand of my righteousness.* Isaiah 41:10

onnie was born Marvin Howard in Lakeland, Florida, to a
father who was killed when Donnie was a young boy. Rev.
Russell H. Sumner, brother to J. D. Sumner, adopted him
and renamed him "Donnie." Donnie was influenced by J. D.,
Roger McDuff, and Jake Hess. He has been told that he has a tear in
his voice like Roger McDuff, pronounces his words like Jake Hess, and
that he has the volume of James Blackwood.

In 1960 Donnie joined the Songsmen, and in 1964 he was with the
Stamps Trio. In 1965 he joined the Stamps Quartet, and in 1972 he
started the Tennessee Rangers. In 1973 he joined Elvis Presley, who
renamed the group "Voice." Donnie was part of an eighteen-man entou-
rage known as the Memphis Mafia, but "Voice" was on call to sing for
Elvis at any time. One night they sang "In the Sweet By and By"
eighteen times. This group also opened for Elvis's shows and performed
his onstage backup vocals.

In 1970 Donnie's song, "Things That Matter," was nominated for
a Grammy Award in the category of Country Song of the Year. That
same year he was awarded the Dove Award for Song of the Year for his
work, "The Night before Easter." Less than a year before Elvis died
in 1977, Donnie left "Voice" and experienced a spiritual new-birth in
his faith walk with Jesus Christ.

Donnie says he has retired from show business for full-time Christian service. He proclaims the good news that "in Jesus there is a new
life, an abundant life, and the assurance of eternal life."

Donnie's favorite song is "In the Sweet By and By."

J. D. Sumner

November 19, 1924—November 16, 1998

For if we believe that Jesus died and rose again, even so them also which sleep in Jesus will God bring with him. 1 Thessalonians 4:14

orn in Lakeland, Florida, John Daniel Sumner was the youngest of four children. His father was a sharecropper in the summer and worked the fruit groves in winter. His mother, a direct descendant of Robert E. Lee, was a supervisor at a grapefruit canning plant. At the age of four, J. D. heard Frank Stamps sing at a camp meeting in Wimauma, Florida, and told his mother he wanted to be a bass singer.

At eleven J. D.'s first pay was a box of candy from WLAK radio, where he sang in a quartet with his sister and cousins. A big break came in 1945 when he joined the Sunny South Quartet. A lifelong friendship developed with the group's lead singer, Jake Hess.

In the late 1940s and early 1950s, J. D. sang with the Sunshine Boys in Wheeling, West Virginia. The group worked out of the WWVA Jamboree and also in Hollywood as singing cowboys in western movies. In 1954 J. D. accepted a position with the Blackwood Brothers, who were at the top of the gospel music world.

In 1965 J. D. joined the Stamps Quartet, whom he had rejuvenated after purchasing the Stamps Quartet Music Company. This group can boast the longest history of any male quartet. The group's theme song, "Give the World a Smile," was carried across the United States and Europe.

Always Elvis Presley's favorite bass singer, J. D. sang with Elvis on tour and in recording sessions.

"There was a lot of love between Mary and me," said J. D. of his marriage to Mary Agnes Varnador. Known as "Miss Mary," she was his constant support as well as business partner.

J. D.'s rare talent and abilities lifted the entire industry of gospel music to national prominence.

—Shirley Sumner Enoch

Tanya Goodman Sykes

October 21, 1959—

O LORD, thou hast searched me, and known me. Thou knowest my downsitting and mine uprising, thou understandest my thought afar off. Psalm 139:1–2

orn in Dallas, Texas, Tanya spent most of her childhood in Madisonville, Kentucky. The daughter of gospel legend, Rusty Goodman, Tanya has gospel music in her blood. At sixteen she was traveling and performing with her family and has been a part of the Goodman Family tradition of inspiring music ever since.

Tanya possesses an impressive vocal ability, one moment tenderly caressing a ballad and the next reveling in a joyous song of celebration. A regular on Homecoming videos, she brings her special style of music that is sure to move all who hear her.

Tanya and her husband, Michael Sykes, penned the number-one songs, "Prayer Warrior" and "The King of Who I Am." She has written and recorded several children's projects, among them the Grammy Award winner, *Rock-a-bye Collection,* and the much-acclaimed, *A Child's Gift of Lullabyes.*

Along with their daughters, Mallory and Aly, Michael and Tanya make their home near Nashville. In recent years Tanya has spent less time on the road and more time attending ballgames, recitals, choir practice, and fulfilling what she believes is the greatest call upon her life, being a mom.

"During my lifetime, I've been able to travel to so many places and meet countless precious men and women of faith. I've had opportunities to do and experience things that I only dreamed of when I was a young girl. My family is my greatest source of joy here on earth, and they are healthy, strong, and seeking after God. What more could I ask? God is good, and I feel truly blessed," summaries Tanya.

Tanya's favorite song is "It Is Well with My Soul."

Russ Taff

November 11, 1953—

Therefore if any man be in Christ, he is a new creature: old things are passed away; behold, all things are become new. 2 Corinthians 5:17

uss Taff grew up in Missouri, in a family where his father was a Pentecostal preacher and his mother loved southern gospel music. Russ and his four brothers learned early that gospel music was the only music allowed in the Taff home. Young Russ recalls standing on the altar, balanced by his mom, singing with much passion the hymns of the church.

Moving to Arkansas in his teens, Russ began listening to contemporary Christian music for the first time and formed a band called the Sounds of Joy. He began to write songs that combined his early church influences with the music of his generation. In the late 1970s Russ was invited to join the Imperials as lead vocalist. His composition, "We Will Stand," became his signature song. After award-winning years with such songs as "Trumpet of Jesus" and "Praise the Lord," he left the Imperials for a solo career.

Over the next twenty years Russ collected three Grammy Awards and nine Dove Awards. *Billboard Magazine* has hailed him as having "the single most electrifying voice in Christian music."

Bill Gaither invited Russ to be a part of the Homecoming videos on a regular basis. In July 2001 when Mark Lowry left to pursue a solo career, Bill asked Russ to become the new baritone in the Gaither Vocal Band.

Russ's eclectic taste is reflected in his live concerts and recordings that include a mixture of southern gospel, rock, pop, black gospel, blues, country, and even big band music.

Russ and his wife, Tori, co-writer of many of his songs, have two daughters, Maddie Rose and Charlotte.

Amber Nelon Thompson

March 28, 1989—

Lead me in thy truth, and teach me: for thou art the God of my salvation; on thee do I wait all the day. Psalm 25:5

 orn in Marietta, Georgia, Amber is the daughter of Kelly Nelon Clark and granddaughter of Rex Nelon; singing comes naturally to this young lady. Amber fulfilled a lifelong dream when her parents offered her the opportunity to sing soprano with the Nelons on a full-time basis. Not only was Amber the most obvious choice to take on this role but also the most qualified.

Since making her first appearance onstage at the prestigious Dove Awards when she was only a week old, Amber has become one of the most recognized artists in gospel music. In addition to being featured on the Gaither Homecoming Kids videos, Amber recently started appearing on the Gaither Homecoming Friends videos and television series.

Amber is a seasoned recording veteran. Her two solo recordings, *Show & Tell* and *Amber & Friends*, were both nominated for Dove Awards by the Gospel Music Association, making her the youngest-ever nominee.

Amber is active in the youth group at her home church, Grace Baptist, where her parents serve on staff. She also enjoys traveling around the world singing with her family, the Nelons.

At her grandfather's memorial service Amber touched the hearts of everyone with her tribute in song, "Amazing Grace." Amber is a third-generation gospel music talent who is surely making her grandfather, Rex Nelon, proud.

—Jason Clark

Jack Toney

August 24, 1933—April 15, 2004

And let us not be weary in well doing: for in due season we shall reap, if we faint not. Galatians 6:9

ackie Alonza Toney was born on Sand Mountain near Boaz, Alabama, to Curtis and Carrie Toney. They took young Jackie to the nearby Baptist church where he learned to sing the old hymns. His love for music and his natural talent were evident as he learned to play the piano, organ, guitar, mandolin, and banjo. He could also sing like an angel.

In the early 1950s Jackie's favorite singer was James Blackwood, who became his friend. Jack began singing professionally in 1951 with the Joymakers and later joined the Prophets Quartet. He toured with the Florida Boys and the Speers, and later became the original lead singer for the Dixie Echoes. In 1963 Jack joined the Statesmen Quartet and toured with them for seventeen years.

In the early 1980s after a number of years in radio and on television, Jack returned to southern gospel music with the Masters V. With Jack as lead singer, the Stamps were nominated by the Country Music Academy as Gospel Group of the Year in 1985.

Jack was a prolific songwriter penning over 600 songs. He received a Number-One Song Award for "I Will Rise Up from My Grave" from the Nashville Songwriters Association International.

In 1996 Jack received the Living Legend Award from the Grand Ole Gospel Reunion. Two years later he was honored as a member of the Statesmen Quartet when they were inducted into the Gospel Music Association Hall of Fame.

Jack enjoyed the many years he spent as part of the Gaither Homecoming family and is featured on many of the videos.

He is survived by his wife, Gail, daughter, Cherie, and two granddaughters, Lauren and Alexandra.

Wally Varner

January 13, 1926—December 28, 2004

But they that wait upon the LORD shall renew their strength; they shall mount up with wings as eagles; they shall run, and not be weary; and they shall walk, and not faint. Isaiah 40:31

Born in Winter Haven, Florida, Wallace Belmont Varner was one of ten children. His dad, Jesse, was a singing convention schoolteacher, and he chose the piano for Wally to play. An old upright piano was purchased for Wally; and, as it turned out, he had a natural talent for the instrument.

Seventeen-year-old Wally joined the navy during World War II. After the war, he played for the Melody Masters Quartet for a couple of years. From 1949 until 1955 Wally's piano style blended well with the Homeland Harmony Quartet. The next group Wally joined was the Revelaires Quartet in 1956. Then he spent a year with the Deep South Quartet in 1957 before joining the Blackwood Brothers for five years.

Many of the awards familiar to us today were not given out prior to 1963. Wally's awards came later. He has been lauded with the Living Legend Award, Gospel Music Piano Roll of Honor, and Gospel Music Association Hall of Fame with the Blackwood Brothers.

Wally's compositions, "Crown Him King" and "Bell of Joy Keep Ringing," have been recognized as masterpieces.

Wally and his wife, Polly, have two daughters, Dale and Debbie, four grandchildren, and four great-grandchildren. Polly continues their ministry with Varner Music, Incorporated, in Winter Haven, Florida.

The songs most requested for Wally to play were "How Great Thou Art" and "Amazing Grace." Wally loved too many songs to be able to choose a favorite. His ministry's motto was "Spreading the Word Through Song," which he accomplished for over seventy years.

Jason Waldroup

December 31, 1976—

I can do all things through Christ which strengtheneth me.
Philippians 4:13

he 1995 National Quartet Convention forever changed the life of an eighteen-year-old from Opelika, Alabama. It was there that Jason Waldroup stood in a stairwell at the Louisville Convention and Expo Center and sang his favorite song, "Victory in Jesus," *a cappella* for Gerald Wolfe and Rodney Griffin of Greater Vision.

Jason enjoyed listening to the sounds of the Cathedrals and Gold City while growing up, and when Gerald Wolfe offered him the dream job of singing tenor with Greater Vision, he said "Yes!"

According to Jason, "No one else in my family sings, so I learned the style of southern gospel music from listening to the groups on the radio. I loved the music, especially Greater Vision. It was truly a dream come true to be a member of this fine group."

Jason Waldroup was saved at the age of fifteen during a revival meeting that his pastor was preaching. He has enjoyed numerous awards and moments with Greater Vision including number-one hits, fan awards, historic appearances, and unbelievable accomplishments.

A fact most fans don't know is that before joining Greater Vision, Jason sang in a part-time group called Faith and Believers for six months. He has been with Greater Vision since 1995. Fans have honored him with the Favorite Young Artist Award and in 2004 presented him with Tenor of the Year during the *Singing News* Fan Awards.

Jason now makes his home in Morristown, Tennessee, with his wife, Missy, and daughter, Abigail.

—Crystal Burchett

Earl Weatherford

October 10, 1922—June 19, 1992

And we know that all things work together for good to them that love God, to them who are the called according to his purpose. Romans 8:28

arl Weatherford was a native of Paoli, Oklahoma. Every afternoon he would hurry home from school, turn on the radio, and listen to the Frank Stamps Quartet. Earl was partial to male quartets. His favorites were the Homeland Harmony and the Blackwood Brothers. It was not unusual for Earl to walk five miles to attend a singing convention on a Sunday afternoon. Singing conventions, common events in those days, emphasized tight harmonies and the blending of voices. Earl learned from these conventions and developed his own ideas about proper quartet singing.

During World War II Earl moved to California to work in the shipyards. While there in 1944, he organized the Gospel Harmony Boys to sing for a local gospel radio show.

Earl met the beautiful sixteen-year-old Lily Fern Goble at a singing convention. She would have a major influence on the future of his group. Earl and Lily were married in 1945, and eventually Lily became a permanent member of the group. Over the years the Weatherfords mentored young talent including Glen Payne, George Younce, Armond Morales, and Henry Slaughter.

After many location and personnel changes, the Weatherfords found a home in Akron, Ohio, with the Cathedral of Tomorrow. As that work grew and required a group to be on staff full time, the Weatherfords chose to continue their traveling ministry.

Earl and Lily adopted two infants, Susan and Steve. Steve took an interest in the quartet. Once when a baritone singer got sick, Steve begged for a chance to sing.

A life of touring took its toll and Earl died in 1992 of congestive heart failure. With the help of others, Lily and Steve have continued in music ministry, making the Weatherfords one of the oldest groups still traveling with original members.

Lily Fern Weatherford

November 25, 1928—

I can do all things through Christ which strengtheneth me.
Philippians 4:13

L ily Fern Goble was born in Bethany, Oklahoma, into a very strict Nazarene preacher's family. At the age of four her family moved to Los Angeles. Lily Fern attended a few Sunday afternoon singing schools and remembers that many of the churches in California used Vaughan and Stamps-Baxter books as their regular hymnals. Because of her Nazarene connection, Lily was familiar with mixed groups like the Speers, but the afternoon singing school was her introduction to quartet-style gospel music.

One afternoon in 1944 when she was only sixteen, Lily met the tall, dark, and handsome Earl Weatherford at a singing school. Lily and Earl became good friends and were married in 1945. Earl was a master singer and patient teacher. He taught Lily to sing with "heavier tones" and to "blend with men." They didn't know at the time that he was preparing her for a career with the Weatherfords. At first Lily filled in only occasionally while they searched for a new member. Eventually, she asked Earl to let her sing as a permanent member.

In 1949 the group began to travel full time in a first-class manner with a 1948 Buick pulling a one-wheel trailer. With no definite destination, the Weatherfords landed in Fort Wayne, Indiana, at radio station WOWO. As a 50,000-watt, clear-channel station with a nationwide reach, WOWO literally introduced the Weatherfords to America.

After a stint at the Cathedral of Tomorrow, the Weatherfords took to the road again full time. Earl passed away in 1992. Today Lily and son, Steve, are keeping the family legacy alive in full-time music ministry.

James "Big Chief" Wetherington

October 31, 1922—October 2, 1973

*It came to even to pass, as the trumpeters and singers were as one,
to make one sound to be heard in praising and thanking the LORD...*
2 Chronicles 5:13

ecause of his Native American heritage, Hovie Lister and Lee Roy Abernathy suggested that James Stephen Wetherington should be called "Big Chief." Reared in Ty Ty, Georgia, Big Chief began his career with the Sunny South Quartet and later sang with the Melody Masters. Big Chief served with honor in the United States Navy during World War II.

After the war he joined the legendary Statesmen Quartet that placed him as one of the greatest bass singers of all time. He later moved to Atlanta and directed his beloved "Golden Stairs Choir" at the Assembly of God Tabernacle. He tried to never miss a Sunday, even though the Statesmen had a busy touring schedule.

Big Chief sometimes stirred up church audiences with his onstage shaking that some considered lewd. It has been suggested that Elvis Presley patterned his style of movement directly after Big Chief and his singing style after another of the Statesmen, Jake Hess.

With his partners, Hovie Lister and Doy Ott, Big Chief owned Faith Publishing Company and J. M. Henson Publishing Company, as well as the Statesmen Quartet. Wetherington also owned the Lodo Music Company.

Big Chief died just before his fifty-first birthday of a heart attack in his hotel room in Nashville. He had been appearing at the National Quartet Convention, an event he was instrumental in helping J. D. Sumner start.

He was inducted into the Southern Gospel Music Hall of Fame in 1997.

Gerald Wolfe

April 1, 1963—

And be not conformed to this world: but be ye transformed by the renewing of your mind, that ye may prove what is that good, and acceptable, and perfect, will of God. Romans 12:2

erald Wolfe was born in Morristown, Tennessee. At age eight he accepted Christ as his personal Savior at a Wednesday night revival meeting. He received his love for music from listening to his mother, Mary, play the piano in their church, and as pianist for the church quartet. Gerald says, "She always wanted me to sing and would buy sheet music of new songs for me to learn for church. My mom always encouraged me to play and learn shaped-note music, which I still use today. Both my parents still love gospel music. I grew up going to concerts and Saturday night singings all over east Tennessee. The groups that had the greatest influence on me were the Happy Goodman Family, the Le Fevres, the Speers, and the Cathedral Quartet."

Gerald fueled his desire for gospel music by packing his bags and traveling. He started his journey with the Dumplin Valley Boys in 1981, then the Dumplin Valley Trio in 1986. He soon took the stage with one of his favorite groups, the Cathedrals, from 1986 to 1988. He toured as a soloist from 1989 to 1990 and now nightly takes the stage with Greater Vision, a group he helped form.

Gerald has received many awards including Favorite Newcomer in 1987; Favorite Young Artist in 1988; and Male Vocalist in 2000, 2001, 2002, 2003, along with numerous group awards.

For songs such as "My Name Is Lazarus," "He's Still Waiting by the Well," and "Just One More Soul," Greater Vision has held continuous number-one spots on the Christian charts. Gerald's favorite song to sing is "There Is a River."

Today Gerald and his wife, Donna, still make their home in Morristown, Tennessee, with their children, Benjamin, Avery, and Casey.

—*Crystal Burchett*

Woody Wright

October 10, 1957—

*And we know that all things work together for good to them that love
God, to them who are the called according to his purpose.* Romans 8:28

 oodrow Wilson Wright was born into a musical family in the small town of Cleveland, Tennessee. His dad, Woody, Sr., was a bluegrass musician and sang baritone in a gospel quartet called the Dixieaires. Woody was an active member of the Cedar Grove Baptist Church and was part of the one-hundred-voice youth choir.

In high school he formed a gospel group called the Woody Wright Singers and traveled around the South singing in churches. Growing up in this environment gave him the Christian foundation that has been a solid source of encouragement throughout his various Christian and secular endeavors.

Woody was influenced musically by Flatt & Scruggs, Jake Hess, Larry Gatlin, the Oak Ridge Boys, James Taylor, Kris Kristofferson, the Little River Band, and the Homecoming Friends.

Some of the groups with whom Woody has sung are the Scenicland Boys; Willie Winn & the Tennesseans; Memphis; Ponder, Sykes, & Wright; Matthew Wright & King; and the Prime Time Country Singers.

Woody's compositions have been nominated for awards by the Academy of Country Music and the Gospel Music Association. His songs "I'm Gonna Sing" and "More Than Ever" have been recorded by the Gaither Vocal Band.

"I am most blessed to live in 'Small Town USA'—Alexandria, Indiana, with my beautiful wife and life partner, Yvonne (Vonnie). My twelve-year-old daughter, Carlie, from a previous marriage is a talented musician and an aspiring actress."

Woody's favorite song is "The Love of God" by F. M. Lehman.

George Younce

February 22, 1930—April 11, 2005

Trust in the LORD *with all thine heart; and lean not unto thine own understanding. In all thy ways acknowledge him, and he shall direct thy paths.* Proverbs 3:5–6

he youngest of five children, George Wilson Younce was born in Patterson, North Carolina, to Tom and Nellie. They realized that their baby boy was an entertainer and enjoyed being his audience.

In 1945 Ike Miller invited George to join the Spiritualairs and suggested they go to Dallas to the Stamps-Baxter School of Music. George was overwhelmed and grateful when his dad went to the bank and borrowed the money. The Greyhound bus ride was lonely, and he couldn't stop thinking about home until he arrived and became busy and thrilled with the music lessons he received from the masters of that day.

In 1954 George sang with the Watchmen and during that time he spotted Clara, the most beautiful girl he had ever seen. On April 27, 1955, he and Clara traveled from Beckley, West Virginia, to Raven Cliff, West Virginia, where George paid three dollars for a marriage license, happy that he was marrying the "coal miner's daughter."

For a short while, they lived in Atlanta where George sang with the Homeland Harmony Quartet, a job he later turned over to Rex Nelon. Earl Weatherford asked him to come back to the Weatherfords, and there he found his niche in the music business.

In 1957 George joined the Blue Ridge Quartet. In 1964 he founded the award-winning Cathedral Quartet, and with his partner and Cathedral co-owner, Glen Payne, garnered success. They were together until 1999 when they retired the Cathedral name.

George enjoyed the Homecoming Videos and Concerts where he and other Gaither friends—Jake Hess, Ernie Haase, and Wesley Pritchard—organized the Old Friends Quartet and continued to thrill audiences. George was a co-founder of Ernie Haase and the Signature Sound Quartet.

George and Clara had five children: Gina, Dana, Lisa, George Lane, and Tara, and three grandchildren.

—Judy Spencer Nelon

Acknowledgments

*T*his Is My Story has been decades in the making. However, I spent fourteen months researching and drawing these artists, the giants of gospel music and those destined to be leaders in the genre. In the making of this book, I have had much help and patience from my wife, Avis. I would still be working on it if she had not supported me.

Judy Spencer Nelon shared her vast knowledge of the people in the industry and helped so much in the research. Special thanks to James Bailey, Tammy Burrell, Donald Boggs, Samuel Collins, David Coolidge, David Dobson (dobsonphoto@aol.com) for the use of Mark Lowry's photograph, the GMA for Doris Akers' photograph, Arthur Kelly, Wayne Kinde, Russ Harrington (studio@russharrington.com) for furnishing many of the photographs for the drawings, George Abiad for the photograph of me for the cover, Christie Stephens, and Michael Stephens.

I especially want to thank the writers who contributed to the book: Judy Spencer Nelon, Lou Wills Hildreth, Moan Blackwood, Celeste Winstead, Crystal Burchette, Laurie Winton, Allison Stinson, Bob Crichton, Gloria Stanphill, Jason Clark, Charles de Witt, Tanya Goodman Stykes, Kris Goodman, Bill Lyles, Jr., Bonnie Morales, Laura Lee Oldham, Nancy Gossett, Faye Speer, Steve Speer, Suzan Speer, Shirley Sumner Enoch, Joy MacKenzie, Jack Williams, and Amy Grant.

In addition, I want to thank the music publishers for their permission to print their songs in the book.

Most important, I want to express my gratitude to the singers who are spreading the Good News in song. —*David Liverett*